BLUEPRINTS
The Infant Teacher's Resource Bank

Jim Fitzsimmons

Rhona Whiteford

Stanley Thornes (Publishers) Ltd

Do you receive *BLUEPRINTS NEWS*?

Blueprints is an expanding series of practical teacher's ideas books and photocopiable resources for use in primary schools. Books are available for separate infant and junior age ranges for every core and foundation subject, as well as for an ever widening range of other primary teaching needs. These include **Blueprints Primary English** books and **Blueprints Resource Banks**. **Blueprints** are carefully structured around the demands of the National Curriculum in England and Wales, but are used successfully by schools and teachers in Scotland, Northern Ireland and elsewhere.

Blueprints provide:
- *Total curriculum coverage*
- *Hundreds of practical ideas*
- *Books specifically for the age range you teach*
- *Flexible resources for the whole school or for individual teachers*
- *Excellent photocopiable sheets – ideal for assessment and children's work profiles*
- *Supreme value.*

Books may be bought by credit card over the telephone and information obtained on (**01242**) **577944**. Alternatively, photocopy and return this **FREEPOST** form to receive **Blueprints News**, our regular update on all new and existing titles. You may also like to add the name of a friend who would be interested in being on the mailing list.

Please add my name to the **BLUEPRINTS NEWS** mailing list.

Mr/Mrs/Miss/Ms _____

Home address _____

_____ Postcode _____

School address _____

_____ Postcode _____

Please also send **BLUEPRINTS NEWS** to:

Mr/Mrs/Miss/Ms _____

Address _____

_____ Postcode _____

To: Marketing Services Dept., Stanley Thornes Ltd, FREEPOST (GR 782), Cheltenham, GL50 1BR

First published in 1994 by:
Stanley Thornes (Publishers) Ltd
Ellenborough House
Wellington Street
CHELTENHAM GL50 1YD
England

A catalogue record for this book is available from the British Library.

ISBN 0–7487–1746–3

Typeset by Tech-Set, Gateshead, Tyne & Wear
Printed and bound in Great Britain.

Reprinted 1995

CONTENTS

INTRODUCTION

This is a photocopiable resource bank for teachers of Key Stage 1 children. It provides basic materials that are used regularly in each area of the Infant curriculum to provide information and to assist in daily organisation and future planning.

The material can be used in a great variety of ways. For example, it can be enlarged for classroom display, incorporated into letters and notices, made into posters, reduced to fix into pupils' own books or made into worksheets. The Teacher's Notes section gives ideas on the possible uses of each page.

Written by experienced classroom practitioners, the material is specifically designed for Infants in both content and appearance and will be an invaluable aid for the busy teacher.

Copymasters 1 to 10: Illustrated numbers 1 to 10

This set of number sheets can be coloured by an adult or by older children to make into a wall frieze or they can be coloured by individual young children to compile into a book of numbers.

Photocopy a set of these pictures to be made into matching cards. Have these coloured by an adult, mounted on card, covered with Contact and then cut out so that the children can use them to match one to one with the pictures in their books of numbers.

Use individual sheets as an illustration on a display table, for example a table of 'twos', where you can display pairs of things such as shoes, beads, pencils and so on.

Copymaster 11: Counting to 10

Use this as a whole sheet for each child to practise counting to 10 forwards and backwards. The trucks on each train strip can be coloured in the same colour or in patterns of colour, e.g. red, blue, red, blue, to show odd and even numbers. You can blank out the numerals on the bottom three trains so that the children can fill them in for themselves.

Alternatively, blank out different numerals in each of the bottom three trains so that the children can use the top one for reference to fill in the missing ones. To do this, copy one sheet and blank out the numerals that are not needed, then use this sheet as a master copy.

You can also show the composition of 100 by cutting out 10 separate trains (forward facing) which can then be mounted or placed on a table in a long line. Each train can be coloured in a different shade to make it easier to see the separate tens.

Copymasters 12 and 13: Ordinal numbers 1 and 2

The first sheet covers ordinal numbers from 1 to 3 and the second covers ordinals from 1 to 10. The children can fill in the missing numerals and words and colour the pictures. The sheets can be displayed with a selection of small items (e.g. toy cars, 3D shapes, books, pencils) that the children can use to put in order. Make some small cards with '1st', '2nd', '3rd', etc. on them and have these on the table for the children to place by the items according to their position.

Copymasters 14 to 19: Shapes 1 to 6

Each of these pages shows a different 2D shape repeated several times within a picture. Ask the children to use one or two colours to colour the shape in question. It will help their visual discrimination if you then go on to ask them to count the number of single shapes of that type in each picture. There is space at the bottom of each page for you to add your own instructions.

Mount single, coloured pictures to display on a 'Shapes' table. You can provide a selection of shapes in coloured paper or the commercially available plastic 2D shapes, so that the children can make and re-make simple pictures for themselves.

Copymaster 20: Shapes 7

This shows the common 2D shapes used at KS1. Using the word bank at the bottom of the page the children can write the names on each of the shapes. You could write the initial letter in each shape as a clue. You can copy two sheets for each child so that they can cut out the shapes from one and then stick them on to the other as a matching exercise. Copy the sheet to be cut up on to coloured paper.

Copymasters 21 and 22: Number lines 1 and 2

The first of these two sheets shows a series of number lines from 1 to 20 and the second shows a number line from 1 to 100. These lines can be cut up into strips which can either be mounted on card for the children to use or can be glued on to the inside cover of a child's own Maths book. The right hand strips on Copymaster 21 are made up of centimetre squares and can be cut up to use for comparative measuring exercises.

Using Copymaster 22, each strip of 10 can be coloured individually and then mounted next to its consecutive strip to form a 100 line. The strips can also be enlarged to use as a classroom display of the numbers 1 to 100.

Copymaster 23: Tens and units place value diagram

This sheet can be photocopied, reduced in size if necessary, and glued on to the inside cover of individual Maths books. You can make several more masters by copying the sheet and blanking out any items you wish the children to fill in themselves. For example, on one sheet you could blank out the words for the numerals and on another omit the numerals 1 to 20. These new masters can now be copied in quantity.

Copymaster 24: 100 square 1 (with numerals)

This can be enlarged to A3 size for wall display or reduced to A5 for inclusion in an exercise book. If you wish to add questions to the 100 square, first copy the square at A5 size, cut this out as a block and glue it to the top of an A4 sheet of paper. You can now write questions or calculations in the space below the square and then copy the quantity required.

Use the sheet for a 'fill in the missing numbers' exercise by blanking out random numbers or whole strips, as described above.

Use the sheet to colour multiplication patterns, e.g. colour every third square in red.

Copymaster 25: 100 square 2 (blank)
The children can complete the square with numbers, colour in strips of 10 in separate colours, colour in multiplication patterns, write the numerals for the multiplication patterns and so on.

The grid can also be used for pattern drawing or for drawing symmetrical shapes, if a medial line is first identified with a thicker black line or a coloured line. You can use the grid to play 'Battleships' or as a grid on which to draw a simple map. For example, ask the children to draw a treasure island on the grid, then to add horizontal and vertical axes and, on a separate sheet, to write a secret message giving the grid references for five lots of buried treasure.

Copymasters 26 and 27: Number words 1 and 2
These show the words for the numbers 1 to 20. Enlarge these sheets to A3 size and use them as a vocabulary display for the classroom. The display can be arranged horizontally with numerals below the words. Alternatively, the sheets can be reduced to fit into an exercise book.

A simple game of chance can be played using Copymaster 26. You will need a number spinner made from card, with the numbers 1 to 10 on it. Each player has a copy of Copymaster 26, takes it in turn to spin and can shade in the box containing the number that the spinner lands on each time. Alternatively, the player can write out the word beneath the word on the sheet. The first player to complete all ten wins the game.

Copymasters 28 to 30: Squared paper 1 to 3
These sheets provide grids of $1\,cm^2$, $2\,cm^2$ and $5\,cm^2$. Use them for symmetrical drawings, early work on area and as graph paper.

Copymasters 31 to 39: Multiplication tables
These sheets show the $\times 2$ to $\times 10$ multiplication tables. They can be displayed at A4 size on the wall. Alternatively, they can be reduced to A5 sized sheets which can be cut up and stapled into book form by the children to make individual tables books.

Copymaster 40: Clocks 1
This shows an assortment of clocks and watches. These can be coloured and cut out by the children and can be used by them to design their own covers for a book on 'Telling the time'. The sheet can also be enlarged to A3, coloured and vocabulary can be added to make a resource poster.

Copymaster 41: Clocks 2
This shows a large smiling clock face with separate hands. This sheet can be glued on to card and then coloured and cut out by the children to make individual teaching clocks. The hands can be fixed on to the clock using a brass paper fastener. (The children will need assistance with fixing on the hands.)

Copymaster 42: Clocks 3
This shows a series of clock faces with numerals, but no hands. You can add hands and ask the children to write in the time below each clock. Alternatively, write the times and ask the children to draw in the hands. It can also be enlarged to A3 and examples of the main times (e.g. o'clock, half past, quarter past, quarter to etc.) can be drawn and written in as an aide memoire to be displayed in the classroom.

Copymaster 43: Clocks 4
This shows a series of blank clock faces. It can be used in the same way as Copymaster 42, but this time the children have to draw in their own numerals. This will help them to remember the positions of the numbers on the clock face.

Copymaster 44: Clocks 5
This shows a series of blank digital clocks. You can add digits and ask the children to write in the time below each clock. Alternatively, write the times in words and ask the children to add the digits.

Copymasters 45 and 46: Months of the year and Days of the week
These sheets can be reduced to A5 to include in children's dictionaries or exercise books or enlarged for wall display as part of the classroom vocabulary bank. They can be made into work sheets by blanking out all but the initial letters of the words. The children can then be asked to complete the lists by making reference to the classroom display.

Copymasters 47 to 50: Seasons 1 to 4
The children can make their own contributions to these pictures by adding animals, vehicles and people in connection with seasonal topic work. These sheets can also be used to write poetry, reportive writing, vocabulary or imaginative stories on. They can be enlarged for classroom display purposes as part of a topic on 'Time'.

Copymasters 51 to 57: Calendar page and Months 1 to 6
You can use these to make a calendar. You will need to make 12 copies of Copymaster 51 and write in the name of the month and the daily date configuration on each. The pictures can be enlarged to A4, coloured in by the children, covered with Contact and mounted on card. The pictures and calendar sheets can then be interleaved and held together with ring binder clips. Punch holes in the top of the pages through which ribbon can be tied to hang the calendar.

Copymaster 58: Daily diary sheet
This sheet is to be filled in on a daily basis, for a set period of time. You may wish to restrict this to the period of a topic. Staple a number of these sheets together and hang them with a ribbon from a hook. Use a new sheet daily and display each one next to the days of the week poster (see Copymaster 46) for reference.

Copymasters 59 to 71: Illustrated alphabet
There are two letters each with an illustration on each page. As part of sounds recognition work, copy one sound picture on to the top half of an A4 sheet leaving the bottom half blank. Ask the children to colour the sound and then draw two or three other things that start with that sound. For emergent writers, write a few

words beginning with that sound on the bottom half of the sheet. They can copy these words and illustrate them.

Alternatively, colour the individual sounds and display them as a classroom frieze. You can also make a set of the sheets into a book so that the children can turn the pages and match them with the frieze.

Copymasters 72 to 76: Upper and lower case alphabet
These sheets can be used in a similar way to the illustrated alphabet. Make a classroom frieze or copy single pairs of letters on to the top right hand corner of A4 paper and staple them together to form a booklet for use as a class dictionary.

Also copy the complete alphabet (Copymaster 76) and use it to paste on to the front of individual dictionaries or English exercise books.

Copymasters 77 and 78: Phonic checklists 1 and 2
Copymaster 77 shows the common consonant combinations and digraphs, while Copymaster 78 shows the common vowel combinations and digraphs. They can be used by you as a sounds recognition record for each child. They can be reduced to A5 to paste into English exercise books or dictionaries or can be enlarged to form posters.

To make a phonic game for more able children, cut out the individual sound combinations, glue each sound on to a separate sheet of A4 paper and give one each to groups of three children. The children have a set time, e.g. 20 minutes, to think of or find ten words starting with this sound.

Copymasters 79 to 84: Colours 1 to 6
The individual pictures can be coloured appropriately and mounted on a backing sheet of their own colour and the set of colour sheets used as resource posters. Alternatively, mount each picture on an A4 sheet of the appropriate colour and use these as the front covers for a small individual books on each colour, e.g. 'My book about red'.

Copymasters 85 and 86: Ruled handwriting sheets 1 and 2
Use these when individual sheets of paper are needed for a special piece of writing. For hand writing practice on ascenders and descenders, use Copymaster 86 which has a dashed mid line for guidance.

Copymaster 87: Music staves
This sheet can be copied and used as it is or cut up into strips to use for short phrases. Mount each stave on a piece of card.

Copymaster 88: Library news
Use this to write the library's opening times, rules, new books, this week's librarians, book reviews and library announcements.

Copymaster 89: Books read this month
This can be used as an individual reading record for good readers or as part of the record keeping for a paired reading scheme. It can also be used as a record of home or library reading.

Copymaster 90: Reading record chart
Use one strip for each child. Add the child's name and keep it in their reading book as a book mark and record. You may wish to write page numbers in the boxes or get the reader to colour in one box every time a book has been completed.

Copymaster 91: Reading awards
Duplicate a small quantity of these and give them out to the children as rewards for good effort in reading.

Copymasters 92 to 94: Nursery rhyme characters 1 to 3
Enlarge these sheets to A3 size and use them for classroom display to encourage visual discrimination. You can also make work sheets or individual mounts for separate rhymes. Copy the composite sheet once then cut the copy up into individual pictures. Mount these as desired and add any writing before copying again.

Copymasters 95 to 97: Traditional story characters 1 to 3
These can be used in the same way as Copymasters 92 to 94, but you can also make story sheets by copying the character and adding a title and a border. For more able children put characters from different stories together and ask the children to imagine how they might react to one another and what sort of an adventure might ensue.

Copymasters 98 and 99: Fantasy characters 1 and 2
Use these sheets as described above, or give each child a composite sheet containing several characters and ask them to cut out the characters they want and paste these on to a story sheet, adding an illustrative background with pens, crayons or chalks.

Use the figures as illustrations for phonic work posters. For example, copy the picture of the witch on to an A3 sheet and add a large 'ch' on the hat in colour. Then ask the children to write words ending in 'ch' on her body.

Copymaster 100: Christmas pictures 1 (secular)
Each picture can be enlarged to A4 size and used as a sheet on which to write greetings, lists, notices, poems, stories and letters to do with Christmas. The pictures can also be used as a base for cards, calendars and posters of Christmas events or coloured to make a border around seasonal work.

Copymaster 101: Christmas pictures 2 (religious)
Use this in the same way as Copymaster 100. Alternatively, the figures can be cut out, coloured, glued on to card and, with a small card prop at the back, can be used in a 3D stable scene. Make a simple stable from a small shoe box. The figures can also be made into simple puppets by glueing them on to card and fixing a plastic straw horizontally to the base of the figure for use as a handle. To make a composite stable picture at the top of a story sheet, copy the sheet once, cut out the figures and then arrange them on a separate sheet, overlapping some to fit them on, and enclose the figures in a stable outline.

Copymaster 102: Easter pictures 1 (secular)
Use this in the same way as Copymaster 100, but you can also use these pictures for general topic work on Spring. Enlarge single pictures to A3 size and write in vocabulary, phonic word lists or titles of topics. For example, write the title 'Spring' inside an enlarged chick picture.

Copymaster 103: Easter pictures 2 (religious)
Use this in the same way as Copymaster 100. For church schools, you could copy a single motif at the top of the page to use as a heading for a letter about religious events.

Copymasters 104 and 105: Symbols of religious faiths 1 and 2
These religious symbols and motifs can be used as appropriate as headings on letters about religious events and on posters and notices around the school. The symbols can also be used to make up work cards or enlarged for use on information posters about various faiths.

Copymasters 106 to 114: Topic pictures
These sheets cover topics on food, sea and land creatures. A single motif can be copied on to a sheet, enlarged for wall display or used to write the topic title inside. Vocabulary can be written beneath the pictures for reference. One picture can be enlarged and a crossword drawn inside it or the pictures can be copied or traced by the children. Using topic books for reference, ask the children to add colour, shade and texture to the drawn outlines.

Make posters for specific teaching points, for example endangered animals, healthy foods, sets of animals from specific habitats, animal camouflage in different habitats, carnivorous and herbivorous animals, land and sea mammals and so on. To do this, copy one sheet, cut out the pictures needed, then glue them in the desired arrangement on a new sheet adding any writing needed and use this composite sheet as your master copy.

Use the sheets as a base for art work in connection with the topic. Show the children how to compose different habitat backgrounds using a variety of media (e.g. chalk, paint, felt pens, fabric, wax crayon, wax rubbings, paper collage) and then colour, cut out and glue on the appropriate animals.

Copymasters 115 and 116: Homes 1 and 2
The pictures from Copymaster 115 can be coloured and cut out, then mounted on small coloured squares around a large map of the world, near to their country of origin. Attach a piece of wool from the picture to the correct country and label the country and the house style too. You can also make up a village, town or city using several pictures. Photocopy a dozen of the African huts, cut them out and mount in village formation on a suitable background with the children's own drawings of people, animals and vegetation. A Western city can be made up with flats and an assortment of houses from Copymaster 116. The children can add shops, factories and religious buildings.

Copymaster 117: 'Minibeasts'
These pictures can be used as the elements of a graph showing the incidence of these creatures in one area, e.g. the school garden, or the creatures observed on a walk in town or country. The pictures can also be enlarged and coloured, using real creatures for observation. Cut out the pictures and mount them on a suitable background showing the different habitats they prefer.

Copymaster 118: Dinosaurs
Enlarge a single picture and use it as a vocabulary sheet on which you can write descriptive or scientific vocabulary, e.g. extinct, herbivorous, carnivorous, million etc.

Enlarged pictures can be coloured, using a variety of media such as brushed paint, pastel, wax crayon or printed paints. The pictures can then be mounted on a large frieze or diorama with a background of mountain, jungle, sea shore or desert. Use reference books to find out which dinosaurs lived in which habitats. You can of course copy several of the dinosaurs that lived in herds or groups such as brontosaurus.

Copymasters 119 and 120: Transport 1 and 2
Use these pictures as illustrations for a traffic survey. They can also be elements of a graph for a transport survey to show how many children have experienced each form of transport. Cut out and mount individual vehicles on card then glue a small box to the back of each so that the 'models' can be used in a 3D display of a busy street or a 3D presentation of the surveys.

To make writing sheets for description or reportive work, enlarge and then cut out individual vehicles and copy each vehicle on to the top of a separate sheet. Use these sheets as masters so that each child can have a sheet about a different vehicle.

Copymasters 121 and 122: Jobs 1 and 2
Each picture can be made into a separate sheet as described above. These sheets can then be used as a master copy for you to make into your own photocopiable work sheets for English, Geography or History based work.

Use enlarged and cut out pictures to show sets of jobs in categories such as outdoor/indoor jobs, jobs which make things, service industries, medical and emergency services, and jobs with children. The pictures can be used to make elements of a graph showing parental occupations or the children's ideas on their jobs of the future. They can also be copied in quantity to make posters or pictures of different work places such as a hospital, street, factory, shop or school.

Copymaster 123: Compass points
Make one enlarged copy for the wall. Then make an A4 copy and blank out the letters of the compass points before making the required number of copies. Ask the children to fill these in using the wall copy for reference.

Copymaster 124: British Isles map
Use this in the same way as Copymaster 123 but this time add the names and locations of major cities and

other reference points in your own region to the wall copy and blank out their names before making the children's copies.

Copymaster 125: World map
Add the names of countries, oceans etc. to one A4 copy of this and then enlarge it to go on the wall. Make the required number of blank copies for the children and ask them to fill in the names using the wall copy for reference.

Copymasters 126 to 130: Then and now 1 to 5
Use these as reference material, enlarged for classroom use, or cut them up to remake into composite pictures of 'Life at this time', showing fashion, homes, transport etc. together.

Make question and answer sheets about each period using one or two motifs as illustrations. Cut up the sheets to form a 'Time line' for reference.

Copymasters 131 to 136: Science pictures
These sheets can be copied whole or the flower, tree and animal pictures can be cut up to use separately. In this way they can be used to illustrate an investigation or for the children to make small reference books or to provide elements of a graph for Science or Maths work.

Copymaster 137: Power sources
Use these symbols as elements of a graph showing power sources used in the home or at school. They can also be enlarged and used to make notices and posters on topics such as safety and conservation. Make small coloured conservation notices, e.g. the water symbol with a caption saying 'Please save water' and mount this near all the taps in the school. Use the electric symbol captioned 'DANGER: do not touch' to put near electric sockets.

Copymaster 138: Earth in space
Enlarge this to make it into a poster, or copy one sheet and add your own Science or English work. Then, using this as the master copy, reproduce as many as are needed.

Copymaster 139: Space
Enlarge Copymaster 138 to A3 size then make several copies of Copymaster 139 and cut out a selection of satellites, a space station or two and a shuttle to stick on to the background to form an outer space picture. Alternatively copy each picture on to a separate piece of paper to make into separate informative work sheets. The children can also make their own moonscape background and then add the pictures to show real events, such as men walking on the moon or a moon buggy travelling across the surface. A black background can be used to mount a rocket or astronauts space walking. Imaginary pictures can also be produced with the children's own idea of a Martian background, aliens and cut out figures of astronauts meeting them.

Copymaster 140: Electrical items
The children can colour in the items which they have at home, have used, are allowed to use or enjoy using. The

pictures can be cut up by the children and remounted on separate pieces of paper in sets depicting use, e.g. for cooking, for entertainment, for communication, for personal hygiene and so on. You can also use cut out pictures to make a safety poster. The children can draw two large backgrounds of a room in a house then place the electrical items on one picture in safe places and on the other in dangerous places, perhaps showing overloaded sockets etc. The children can then compare the pictures.

Copymaster 141: The open body
To make a work sheet without the body parts named, make a single copy then blank out the labels and draw a large box in each place so that when you copy this the children can write in the labels themselves using a master sheet with the words in place for reference. Alternatively write the words on the board or on the bottom of your unlabelled master copy. To make a display poster, enlarge the sheet to A3, colour and mount on a piece of coloured paper.

Copymaster 142: The human skeleton
For more able children, use this sheet in the same way as above. You can also make a visual aid that shows the inside of the body as follows. Copy this sheet and Copymaster 141 to A3 size and colour each. Add an A3 sheet of thin white paper to the top and staple all three together at the top. Now trace the outline of the open body on the top sheet and add colour features and clothes to this. This can be stapled by its top edge to a display board for the children to lift the flaps to see inside the body. You can cut round the edge of the top body to make a body-shaped book. This will cut off the labels, but the labelled pictures can be displayed alongside for reference. To make individual body books, copy the sheets at A5 size for ease of handling.

Copymaster 143: Musical instruments
Cut out the separate instruments and ask the children to sort them and stick them on to separate sheets showing those which are blown, plucked or banged to produce the sound. Use the pictures as elements of a graph to show which sounds are preferred by the class or which instruments they have heard played.

Copymaster 144: Colours of the rainbow
The children can colour this sheet to help them remember the colour configuration. It can be used as an imaginative writing sheet if copied at A5 size at the top of an A4 sheet and the children can do verse, description or imaginative writing with the rainbow as inspiration. The sheet can also be copied in this way for Science work on light, using the bottom of the sheet for you to add your own sentences or for drawings of experiments using prisms etc.

Copymaster 145: Special event letter heading
This letter heading should be used sparingly during the year for letters to parents about sponsored events, performances, meetings or demonstrations. Copy one sheet then type out the letter on it and copy this in quantity.

Copymaster 146: Teacher's message heading
Use this for essential short messages to be sent home, such as arrangements for cooking, swimming and regular outings. To make two shorter sheets on one master, copy one sheet and cut off the top heading, place this half way down the master sheet in the book and copy this. Cut the finished pages in half for use.

Copymasters 147 and 148: Illustrated name tags
These provide a collection of illustrated name tags to be used for different organisational purposes. Copy each sheet once as a master and write on each label the name of one child in the class, allocating each child one picture. Use them at this size for cloakroom and shoe store labels. Each sheet can be enlarged to A3 and then these matching larger labels used to stick on to the front of all the child's exercise books and other personal items such as a carrying envelope used to take reading books home.

Copymaster 149: Merit stickers
Make a few copies of this and cut them up to have them available for daily use. Keep a glue stick in the sticker box too.

Copymaster 150: Award certificates
Each of the certificates can be enlarged to A4 if desired. Keep a small store available for class use. They can be adapted to cover achievements in different subject areas or awarded for good behaviour or hard work.

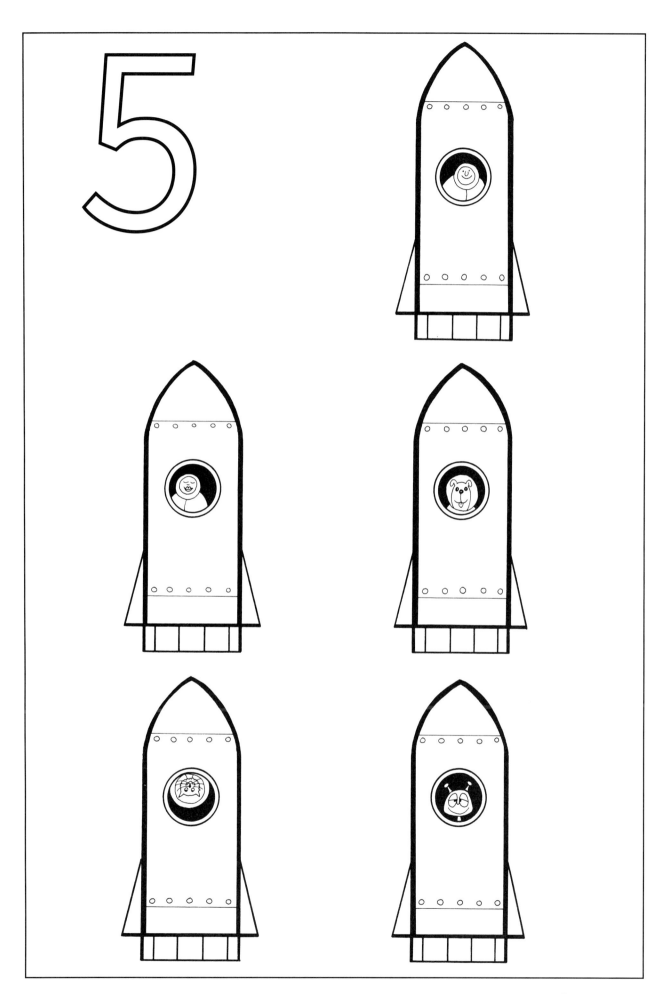

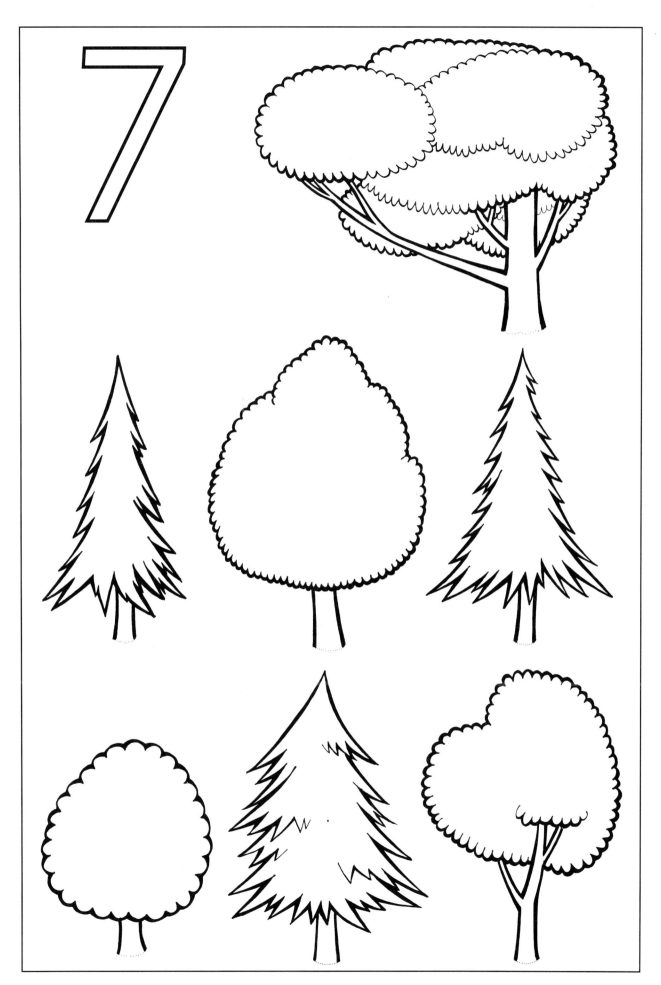

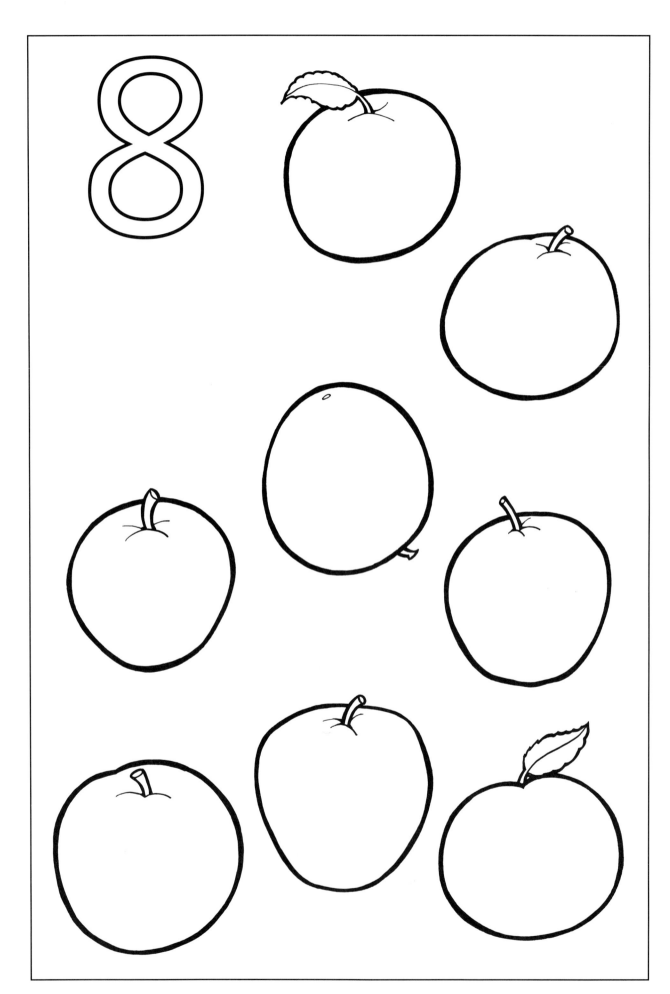

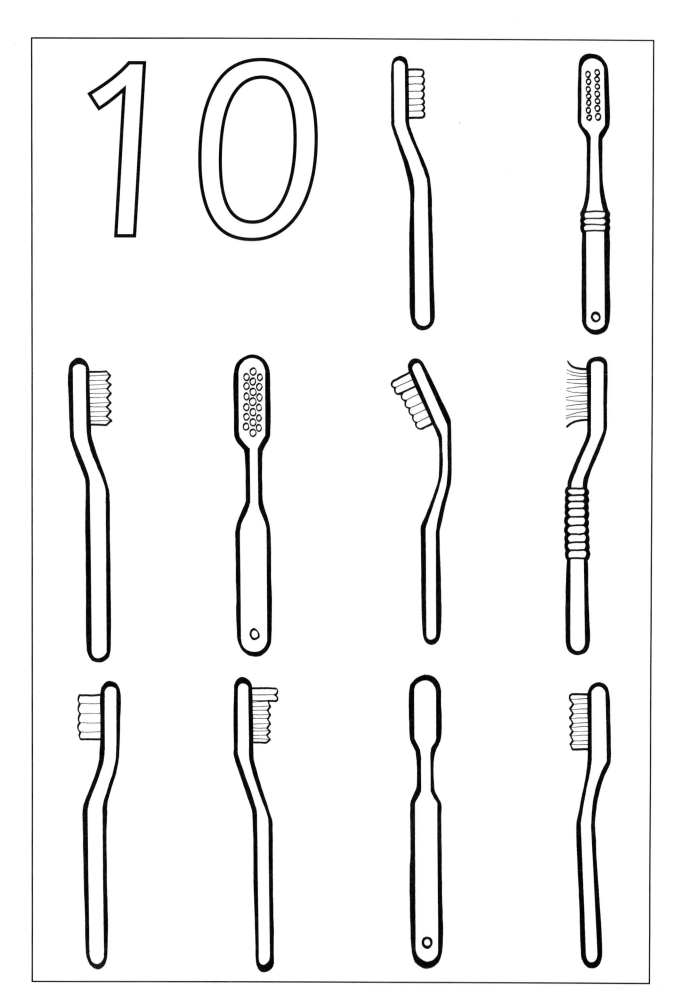

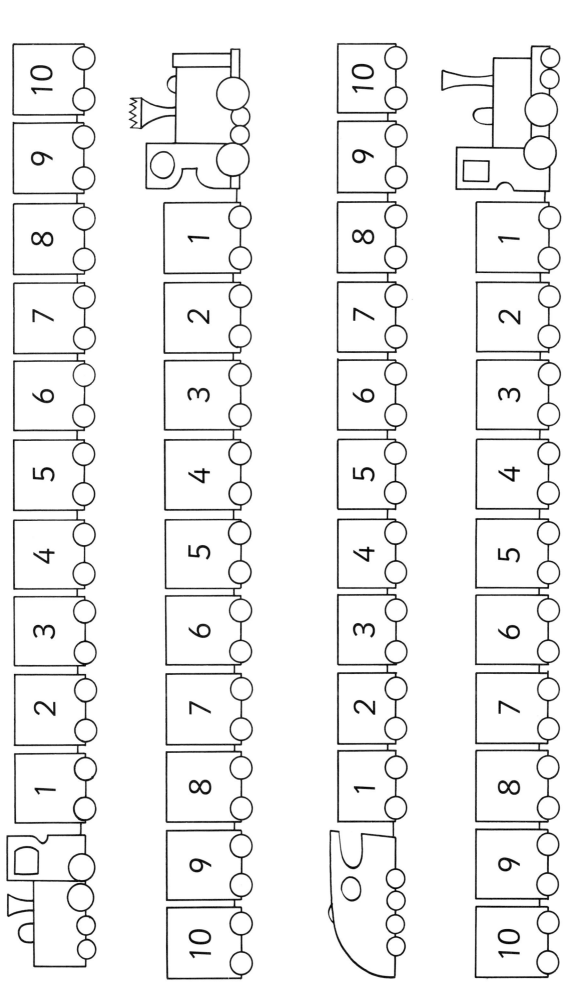

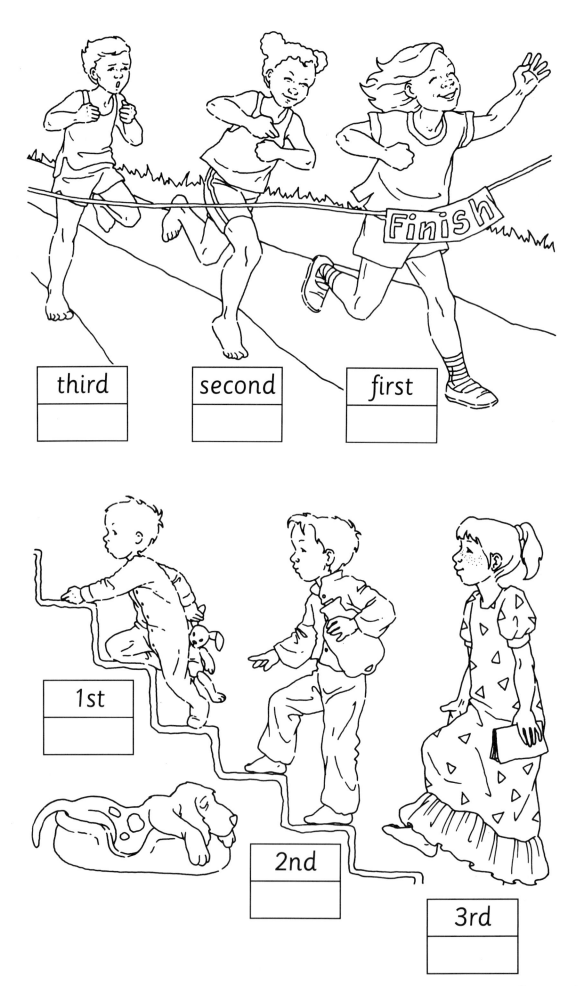

third

second

first

1st

2nd

3rd

1st

5th

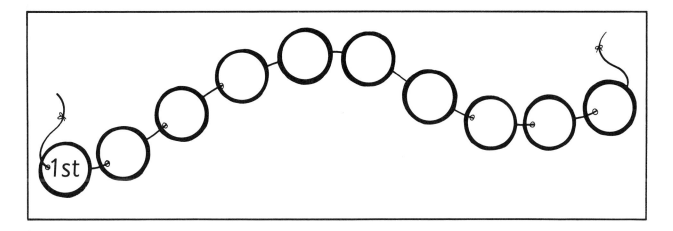

1st

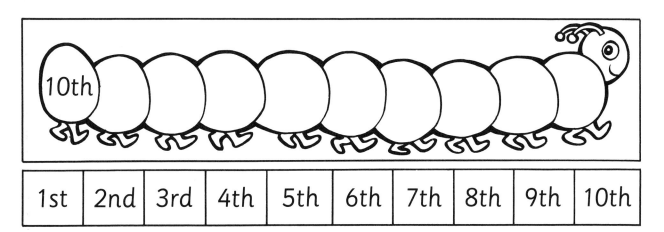

10th

| 1st | 2nd | 3rd | 4th | 5th | 6th | 7th | 8th | 9th | 10th |

Triangle

Circle

Square

Rectangle

Hexagon

Diamond

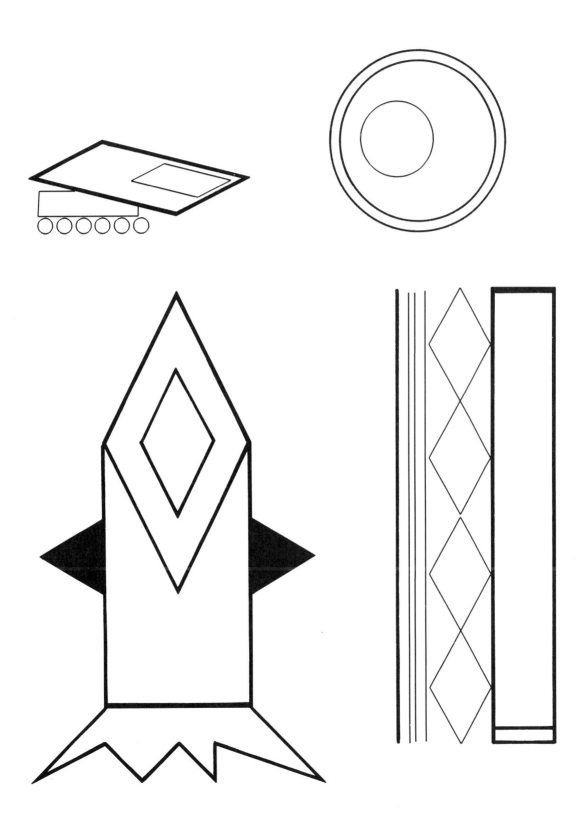

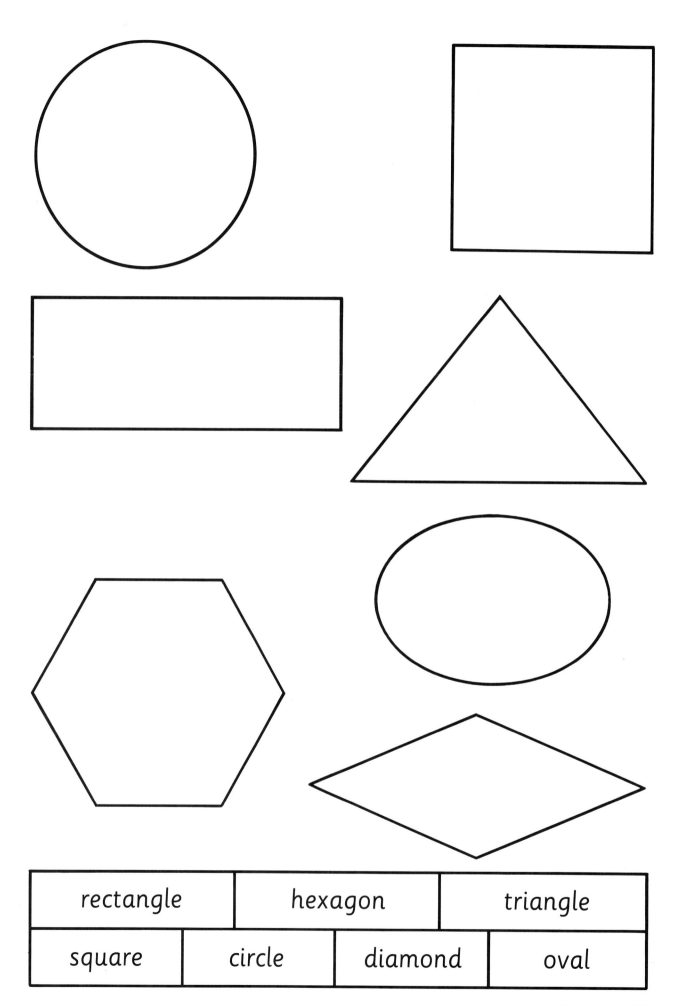

rectangle	hexagon	triangle

square	circle	diamond	oval

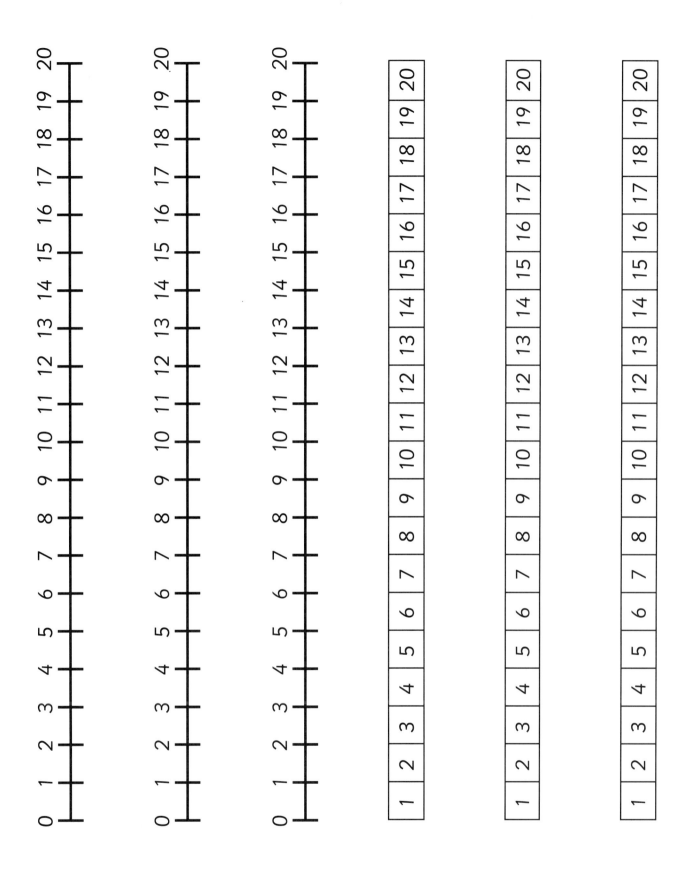

1	2	3	4	5	6	7	8	9	10

11	12	13	14	15	16	17	18	19	20

21	22	23	24	25	26	27	28	29	30

31	32	33	34	35	36	37	38	39	40

41	42	43	44	45	46	47	48	49	50

51	52	53	54	55	56	57	58	59	60

61	62	63	64	65	66	67	68	69	70

71	72	73	74	75	76	77	78	79	80

81	82	83	84	85	86	87	88	89	90

91	92	93	94	95	96	97	98	99	100

Tens and units

I	1 unit = 1 = one
II	2 units = 2 = two
III	3 units = 3 = three
IIII	4 units = 4 = four
IIIII	5 units = 5 = five
IIIIII	6 units = 6 = six
IIIIIII	7 units = 7 = seven
IIIIIIII	8 units = 8 = eight
IIIIIIIII	9 units = 9 = nine
IIIIIIIIII	1 ten and 0 units = 10 = ten
IIIIIIIIII I	1 ten and 1 unit = 11 = eleven
IIIIIIIIII II	1 ten and 2 units = 12 = twelve
IIIIIIIIII III	1 ten and 3 units = 13 = thirteen
IIIIIIIIII IIII	1 ten and 4 units = 14 = fourteen
IIIIIIIIII IIIII	1 ten and 5 units = 15 = fifteen
IIIIIIIIII IIIIII	1 ten and 6 units = 16 = sixteen
IIIIIIIIII IIIIIII	1 ten and 7 units = 17 = seventeen
IIIIIIIIII IIIIIIII	1 ten and 8 units = 18 = eighteen
IIIIIIIIII IIIIIIIII	1 ten and 9 units = 19 = nineteen
IIIIIIIIII IIIIIIIIII	2 tens and 0 units = 20 = twenty

100 square 1

1	2	3	4	5	6	7	8	9	10
11	12	13	14	15	16	17	18	19	20
21	22	23	24	25	26	27	28	29	30
31	32	33	34	35	36	37	38	39	40
41	42	43	44	45	46	47	48	49	50
51	52	53	54	55	56	57	58	59	60
61	62	63	64	65	66	67	68	69	70
71	72	73	74	75	76	77	78	79	80
81	82	83	84	85	86	87	88	89	90
91	92	93	94	95	96	97	98	99	100

100 square 2

one	two
three	four
five	six
seven	eight
nine	ten

eleven	twelve
thirteen	fourteen
fifteen	sixteen
seventeen	eighteen
nineteen	twenty

2× Table

$$0 \times 2 = 0$$

$$1 \times 2 = 2$$

$$2 \times 2 = 4$$

$$3 \times 2 = 6$$

$$4 \times 2 = 8$$

$$5 \times 2 = 10$$

$$6 \times 2 = 12$$

$$7 \times 2 = 14$$

$$8 \times 2 = 16$$

$$9 \times 2 = 18$$

$$10 \times 2 = 20$$

$$11 \times 2 = 22$$

$$12 \times 2 = 24$$

3× Table

$$0 \times 3 = 0$$
$$1 \times 3 = 3$$
$$2 \times 3 = 6$$
$$3 \times 3 = 9$$
$$4 \times 3 = 12$$
$$5 \times 3 = 15$$
$$6 \times 3 = 18$$
$$7 \times 3 = 21$$
$$8 \times 3 = 24$$
$$9 \times 3 = 27$$
$$10 \times 3 = 30$$
$$11 \times 3 = 33$$
$$12 \times 3 = 36$$

4× Table

$$0 \times 4 = 0$$
$$1 \times 4 = 4$$
$$2 \times 4 = 8$$
$$3 \times 4 = 12$$
$$4 \times 4 = 16$$
$$5 \times 4 = 20$$
$$6 \times 4 = 24$$
$$7 \times 4 = 28$$
$$8 \times 4 = 32$$
$$9 \times 4 = 36$$
$$10 \times 4 = 40$$
$$11 \times 4 = 44$$
$$12 \times 4 = 48$$

5× Table

$$0 \times 5 = 0$$

$$1 \times 5 = 5$$

$$2 \times 5 = 10$$

$$3 \times 5 = 15$$

$$4 \times 5 = 20$$

$$5 \times 5 = 25$$

$$6 \times 5 = 30$$

$$7 \times 5 = 35$$

$$8 \times 5 = 40$$

$$9 \times 5 = 45$$

$$10 \times 5 = 50$$

$$11 \times 5 = 55$$

$$12 \times 5 = 60$$

6× Table

$0 \times 6 = 0$

$1 \times 6 = 6$

$2 \times 6 = 12$

$3 \times 6 = 18$

$4 \times 6 = 24$

$5 \times 6 = 30$

$6 \times 6 = 36$

$7 \times 6 = 42$

$8 \times 6 = 48$

$9 \times 6 = 54$

$10 \times 6 = 60$

$11 \times 6 = 66$

$12 \times 6 = 72$

7× **Table**

$$0 \times 7 = 0$$

$$1 \times 7 = 7$$

$$2 \times 7 = 14$$

$$3 \times 7 = 21$$

$$4 \times 7 = 28$$

$$5 \times 7 = 35$$

$$6 \times 7 = 42$$

$$7 \times 7 = 49$$

$$8 \times 7 = 56$$

$$9 \times 7 = 63$$

$$10 \times 7 = 70$$

$$11 \times 7 = 77$$

$$12 \times 7 = 84$$

8× Table

$$0 \times 8 = 0$$

$$1 \times 8 = 8$$

$$2 \times 8 = 16$$

$$3 \times 8 = 24$$

$$4 \times 8 = 32$$

$$5 \times 8 = 40$$

$$6 \times 8 = 48$$

$$7 \times 8 = 56$$

$$8 \times 8 = 64$$

$$9 \times 8 = 72$$

$$10 \times 8 = 80$$

$$11 \times 8 = 88$$

$$12 \times 8 = 96$$

9× Table

$$0 \times 9 = 0$$
$$1 \times 9 = 9$$
$$2 \times 9 = 18$$
$$3 \times 9 = 27$$
$$4 \times 9 = 36$$
$$5 \times 9 = 45$$
$$6 \times 9 = 54$$
$$7 \times 9 = 63$$
$$8 \times 9 = 72$$
$$9 \times 9 = 81$$
$$10 \times 9 = 90$$
$$11 \times 9 = 99$$
$$12 \times 9 = 108$$

10× Table

$$0 \times 10 = 0$$

$$1 \times 10 = 10$$

$$2 \times 10 = 20$$

$$3 \times 10 = 30$$

$$4 \times 10 = 40$$

$$5 \times 10 = 50$$

$$6 \times 10 = 60$$

$$7 \times 10 = 70$$

$$8 \times 10 = 80$$

$$9 \times 10 = 90$$

$$10 \times 10 = 100$$

$$11 \times 10 = 110$$

$$12 \times 10 = 120$$

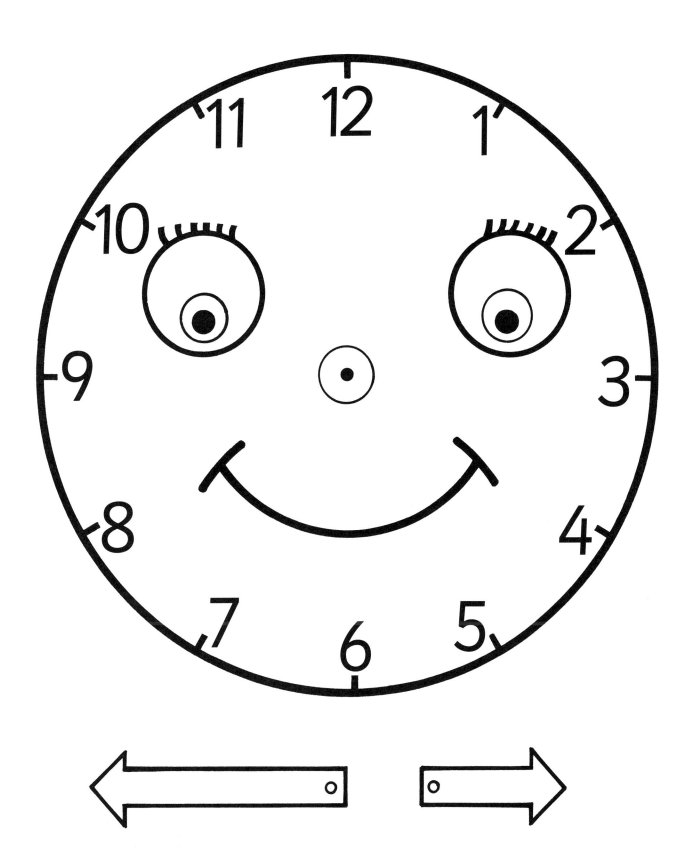

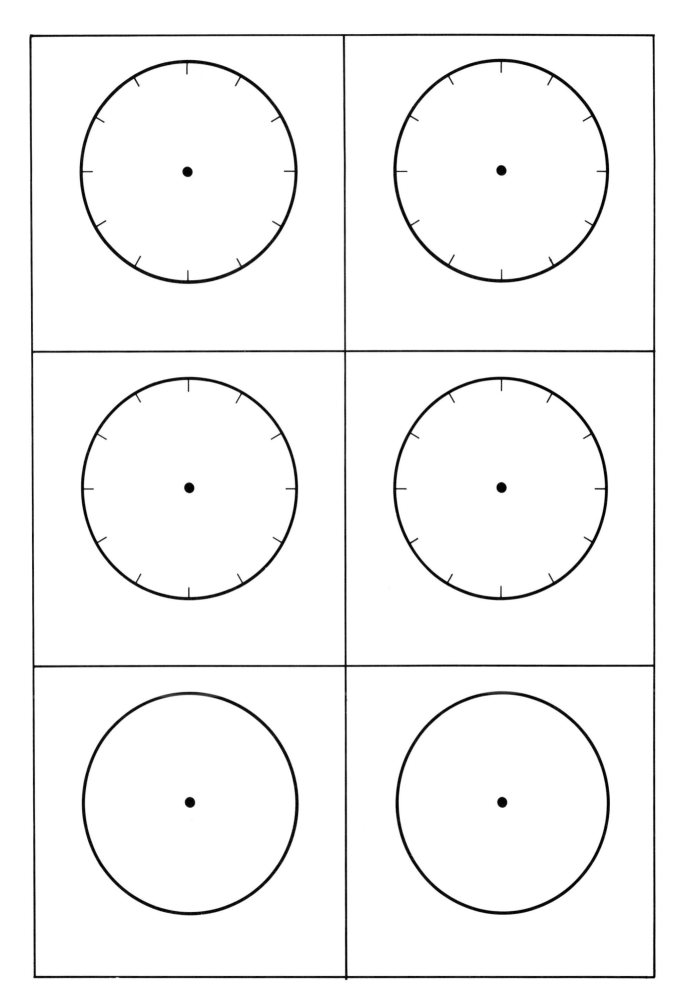

Months of the year

January	1
February	2
March	3
April	4
May	5
June	6
July	7
August	8
September	9
October	10
November	11
December	12

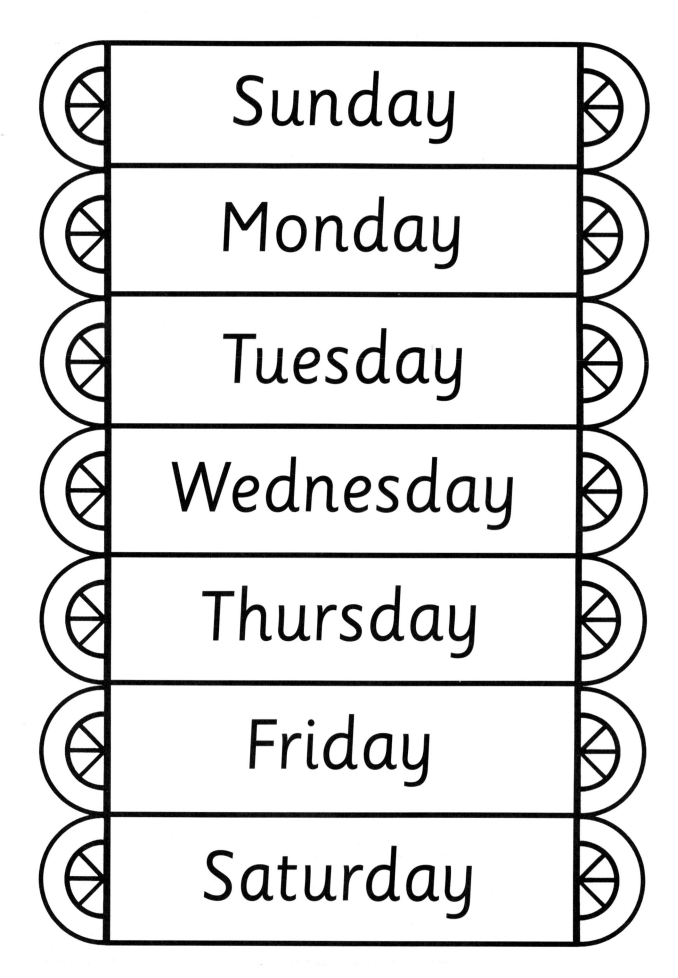

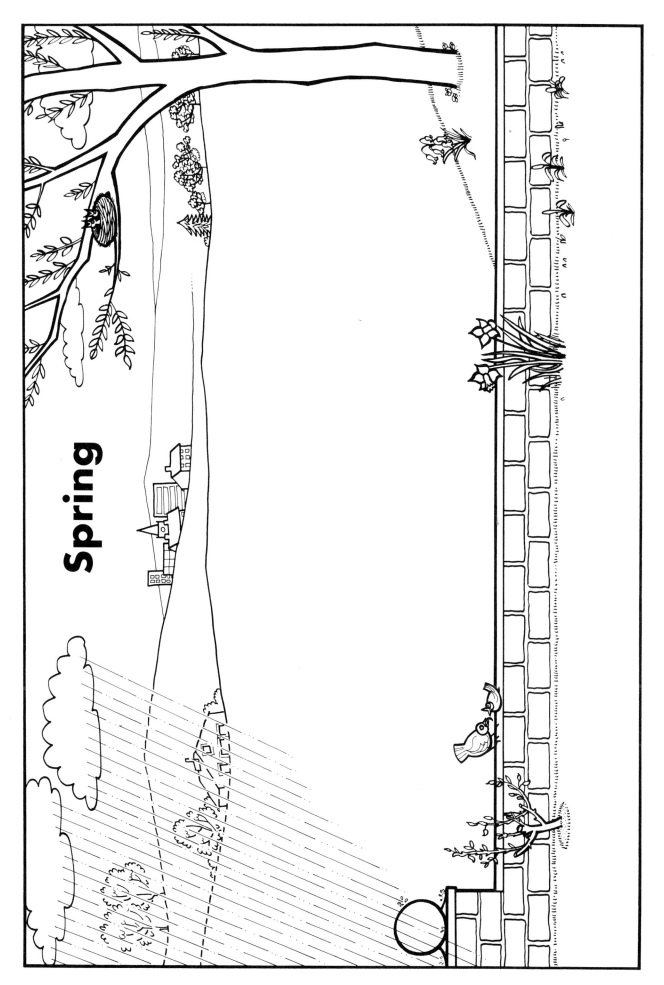

Spring

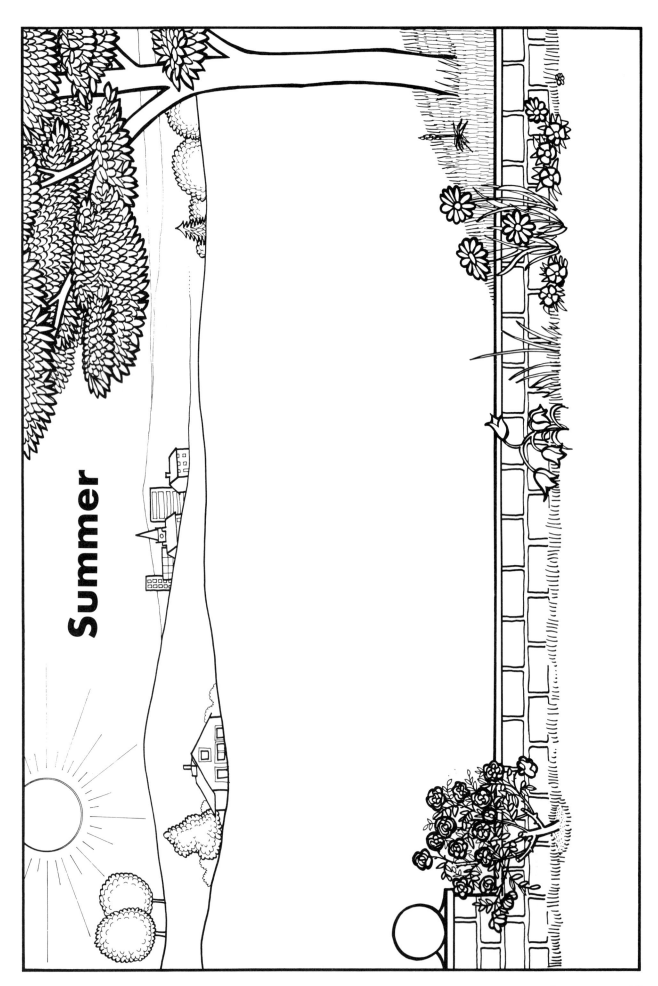

Summer

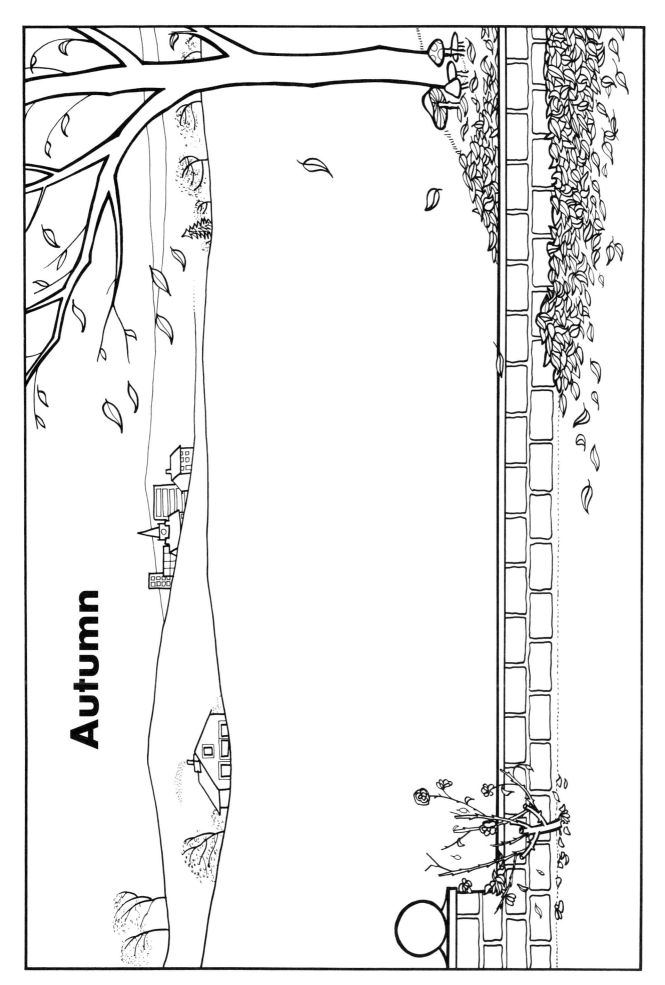

Autumn

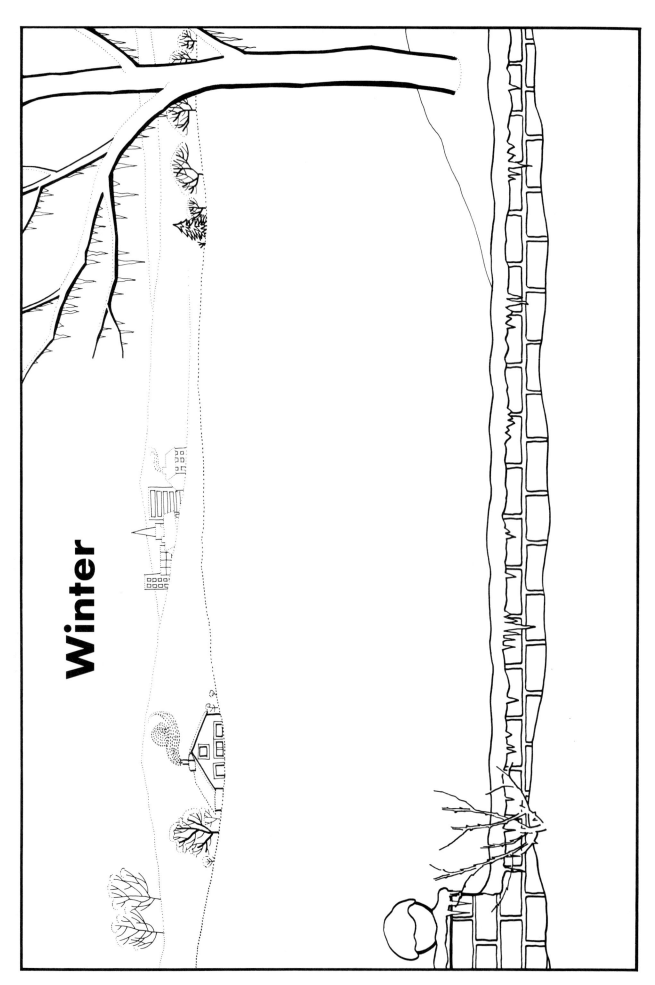

Winter

Sunday	Monday	Tuesday	Wednesday	Thursday	Friday	Saturday

January

February

March

April

Bus Stop

May

June

July

August

September

October

November

December

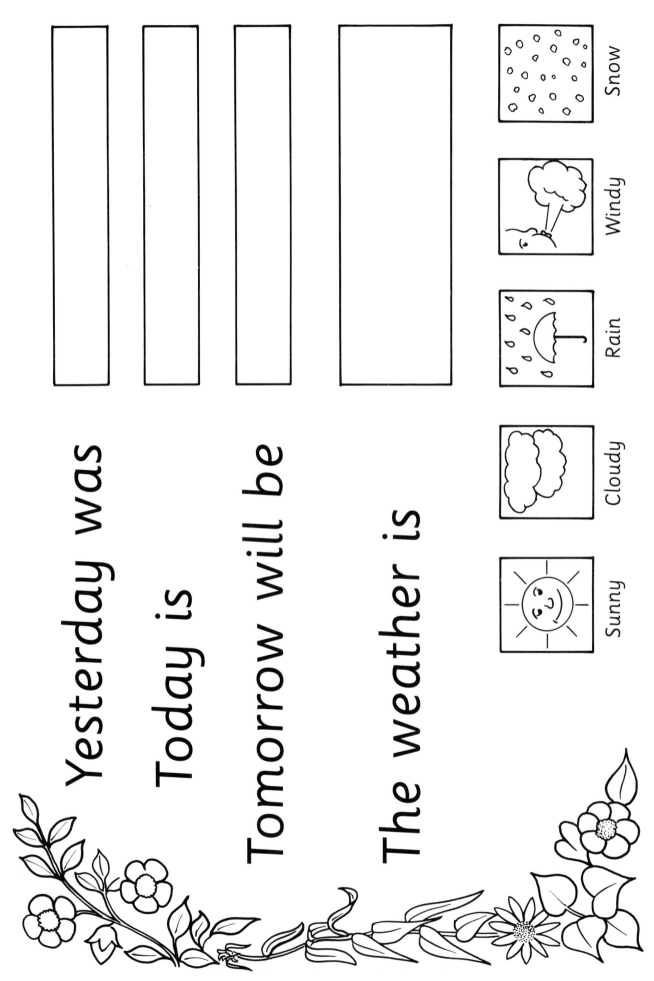

Yesterday was

Today is

Tomorrow will be

The weather is

Snow

Windy

Rain

Cloudy

Sunny

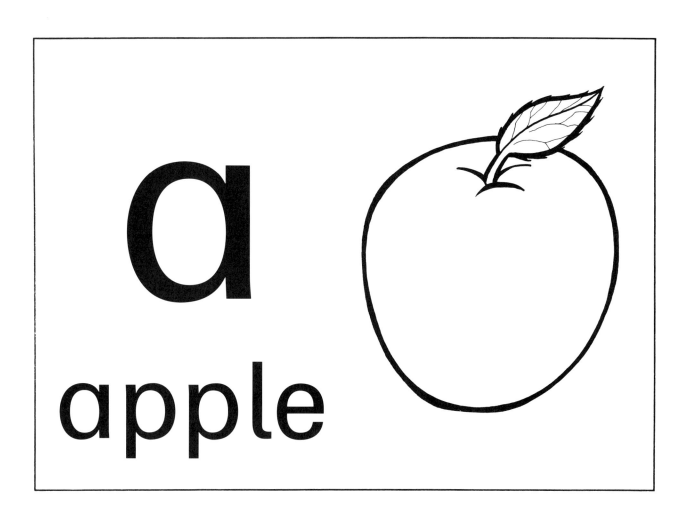

a
apple

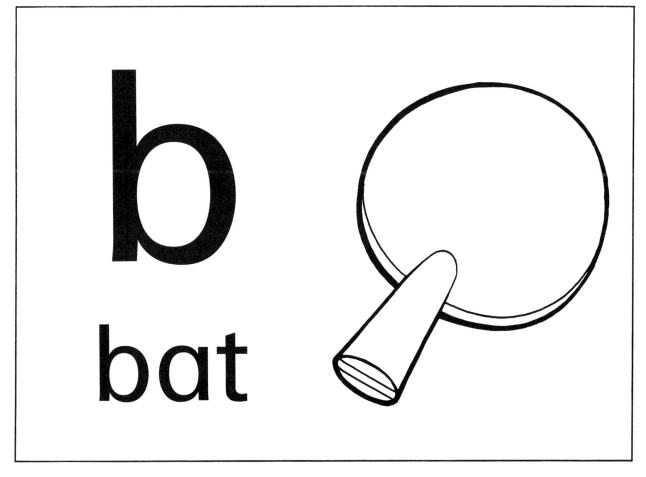

b
bat

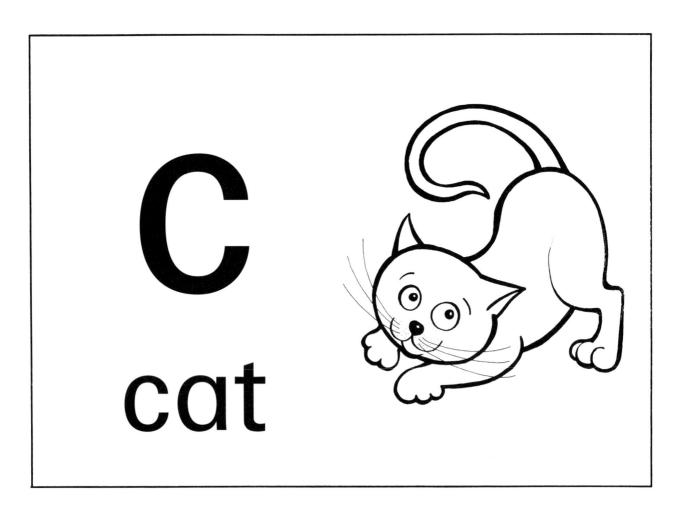

C
cat

d
dog

e elephant

f feather

g

girl

h

house

i
insects

j
jelly

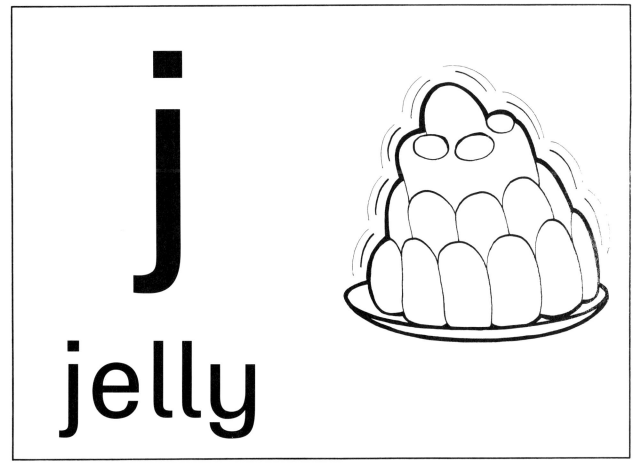

k
kettle

l
leg

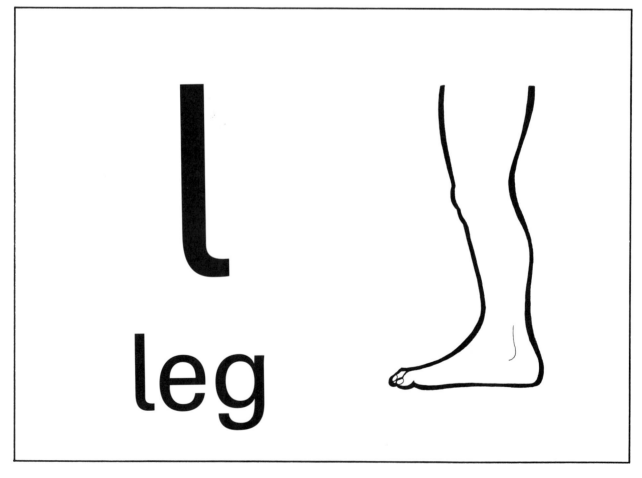

m

mouse

n

nest

o
ostrich

p
pig

q
quilt

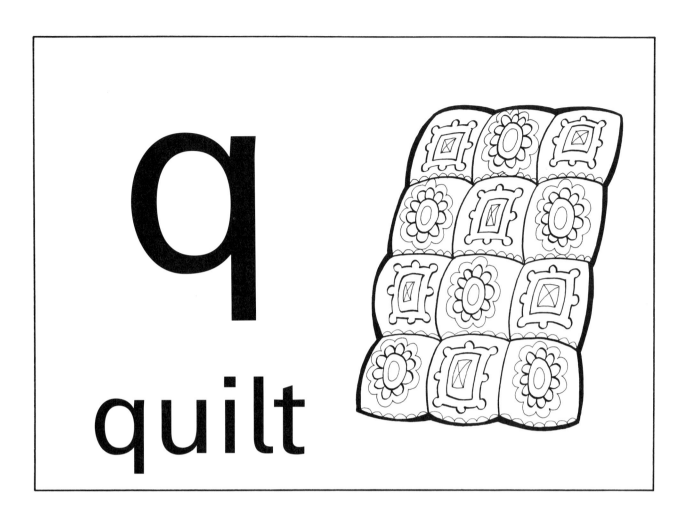

r
robin

s

sun

t

teddy

u
umbrella

v
van

W

whale

X

fo<u>x</u>

y

yacht

z

zebra

Aa	Bb
Cc	Dd
Ee	Ff

Gg	Hh
Ii	Jj
Kk	Ll

Mm	Nn
Oo	Pp
Qq	Rr

Ss	Tt
Uu	Vv
Ww	Xx

Yy Zz

A B C D E F G H I J
K L M N O P Q R S T
U V W X Y Z

a b c d e f g h i j
k l m n p q r s t u
v w x y z

bl	fl	cl	gl
pl	sl	sc	sm
sp	sk	sw	st
gr	cr	dr	tr
nd	nt	nk	st
sk	mp	ck	ll
ff	ss	th	ch
sh	kn	ph	qu

ee	oo	ea (as in head)	ea (as in neat)
ow (as in down)	ow (as in snow)	oa	oi
oy	ou	ay	ai
a_e	o_e	i_e	u_e
er	aw	or	ear
ir	ar	ie	ur
ui	au	ew	

black

white

red

blue

green

yellow

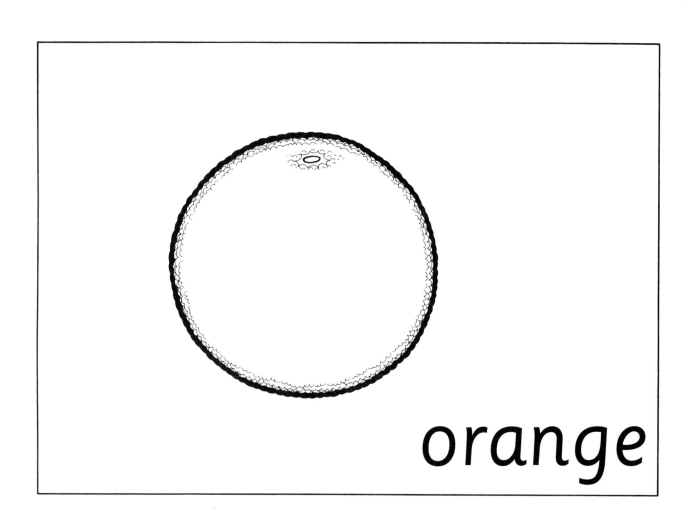

orange

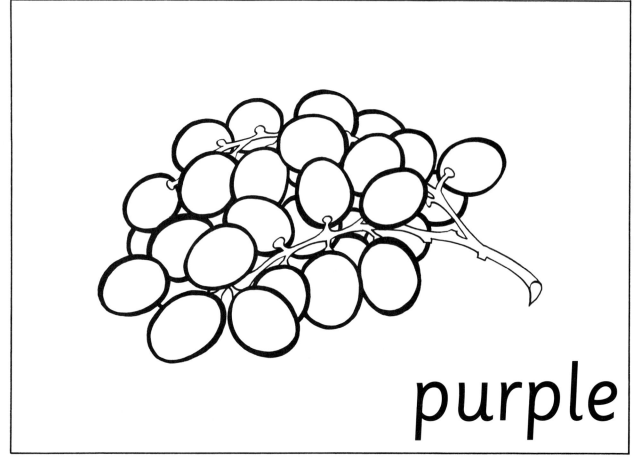

purple

pink

brown

turquoise

grey

Ruled handwriting sheet 1

Ruled handwriting sheet 2

Music staves

Library News

Books I have read this month

1 _____

2 _____

3 _____

4 _____

5 _____

6 _____

7 _____

8 _____

9 _____

10 _____

My favourite was number ☐

by _____

READING AWARD

FOR

_____

WHO HAS _____

SIGNED _____ DATE _____

Super reader

awarded to _____

date _____

by _____

Jack and Jill

Hey diddle diddle

Hickety pickety
my black hen

The Queen of Hearts

Humpty Dumpty

baa
baa

Baa baa black sheep

Sing a song of sixpence

Goosey goosey gander

Hickory dickory dock

Little Miss Muffet

Little Boy Blue

Old Mother Hubbard

Ding dong bell, Pussy's in the well

Rub a dub dub, three men in a tub

Little Bo Peep

Mary, Mary quite contrary

Wee Willie Winkie

Pat-a-cake, pat-a-cake baker's man

Snow White

Little Red Riding Hood

Cinderella

Puss in boots

The three bears

Hansel and Gretel

The little mermaid

Sleeping beauty

The ugly duckling

Jack and the beanstalk

The three little pigs

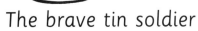

The brave tin soldier

Aladdin

Witch

Wizard

Fairy

Snowman

Genie

Queen

King

Giant

Dragon

Super hero

Calvary

The Paschal candle

The risen Christ

Dove of peace

Menorah – temple candlestick
(Jewish)

Crescent
and star
(Islamic)

Cross
(Christian)

Sword and
bracelet
(Sikh)

Lion of Judah
(Rastafarian)

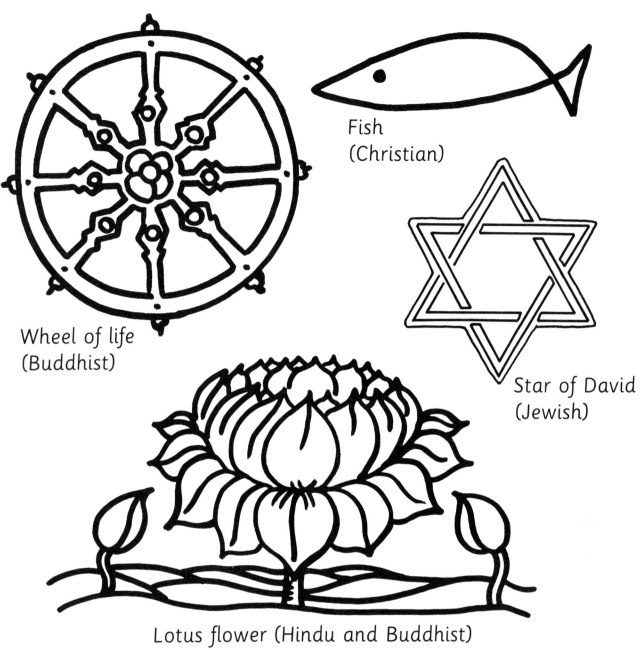

Fish
(Christian)

Wheel of life
(Buddhist)

Star of David
(Jewish)

Lotus flower (Hindu and Buddhist)

Peacock
(Hindu)

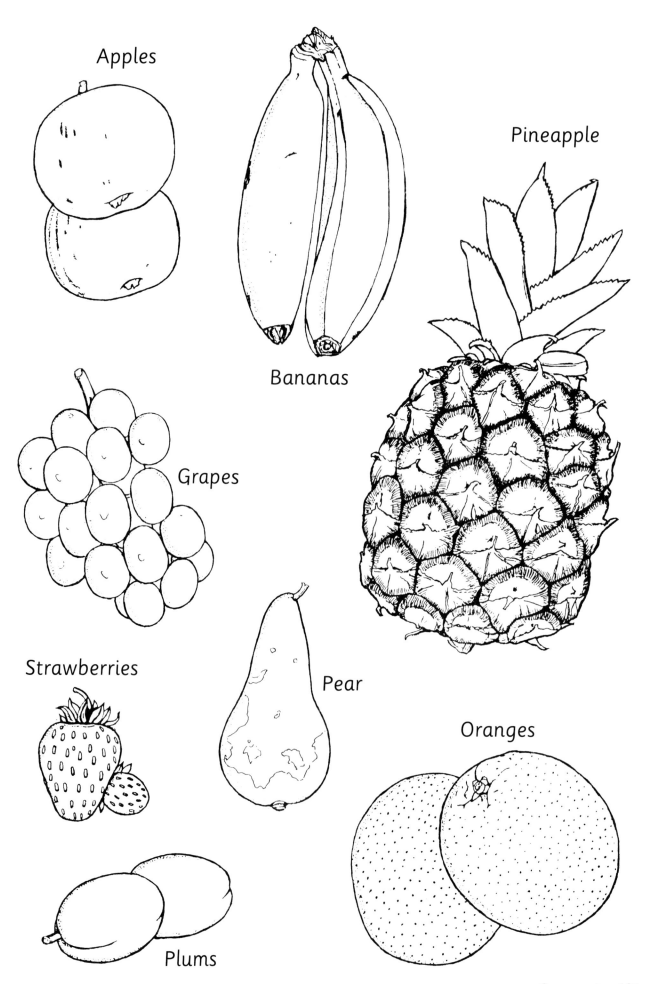

Apples

Bananas

Pineapple

Grapes

Strawberries

Pear

Oranges

Plums

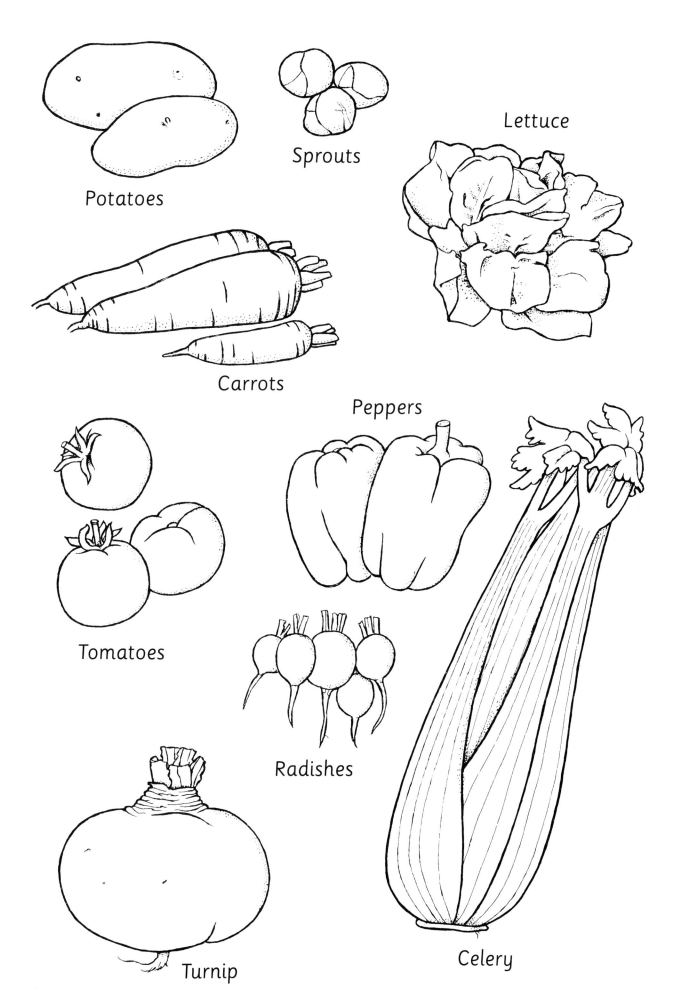

Potatoes

Sprouts

Lettuce

Carrots

Peppers

Tomatoes

Radishes

Turnip

Celery

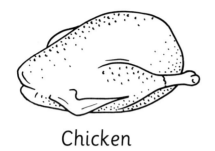

Chicken

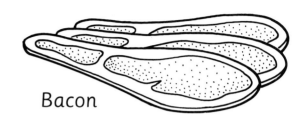

Bacon

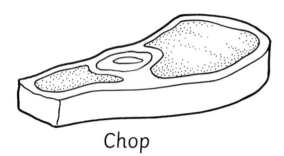

Chop

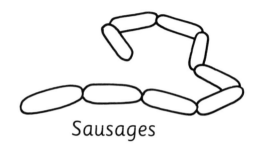

Sausages

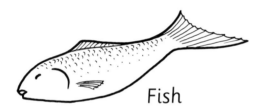

Fish

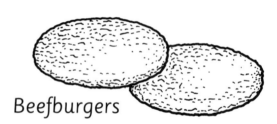

Beefburgers

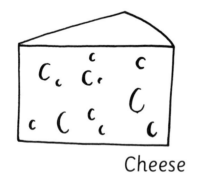

Cheese

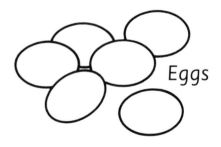

Eggs

Milk

Yoghurt

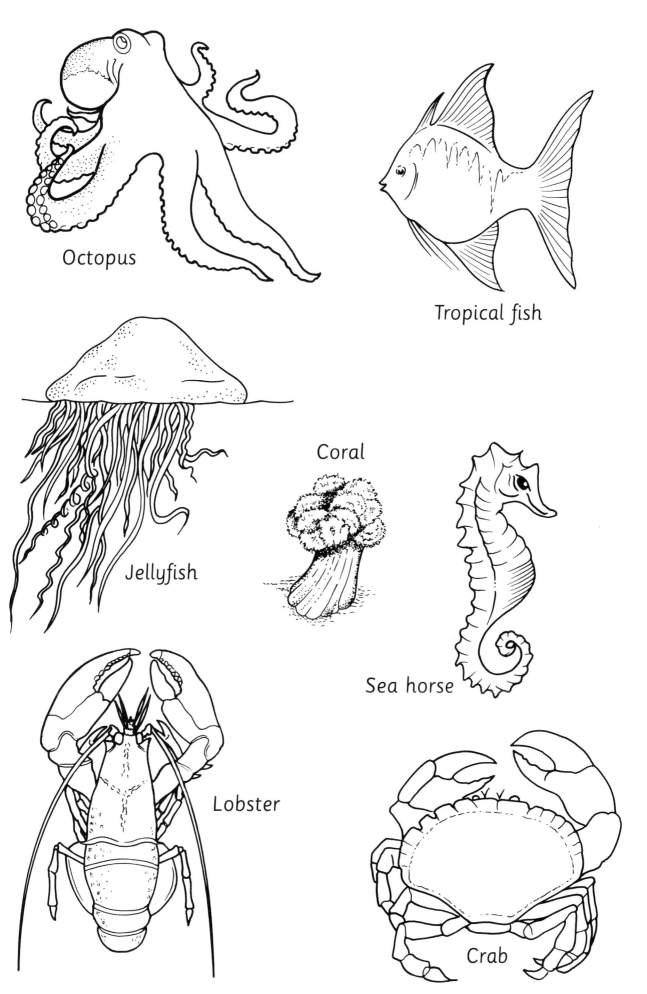

Octopus

Tropical fish

Jellyfish

Coral

Sea horse

Lobster

Crab

Starfish

Sea anemone

Eel

Mackerel

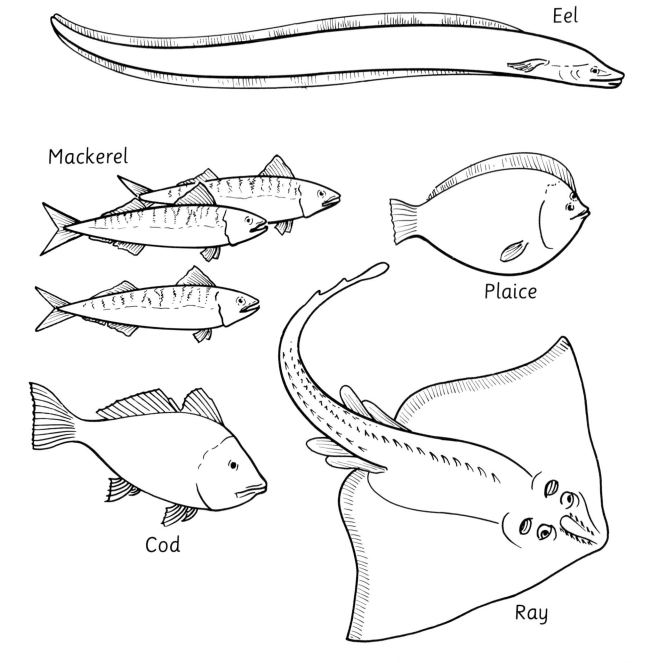

Plaice

Cod

Ray

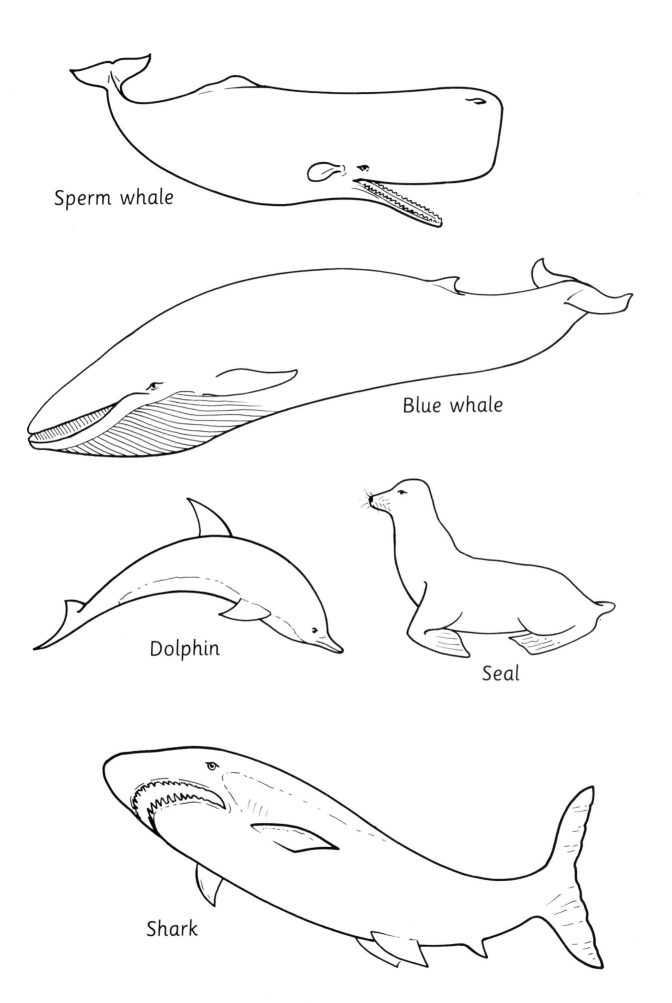

Sperm whale

Blue whale

Dolphin

Seal

Shark

Elephant

Giraffe

Tiger

Gorilla

Crocodile

Ostrich

Camel

Lion

Kangaroo

Snake

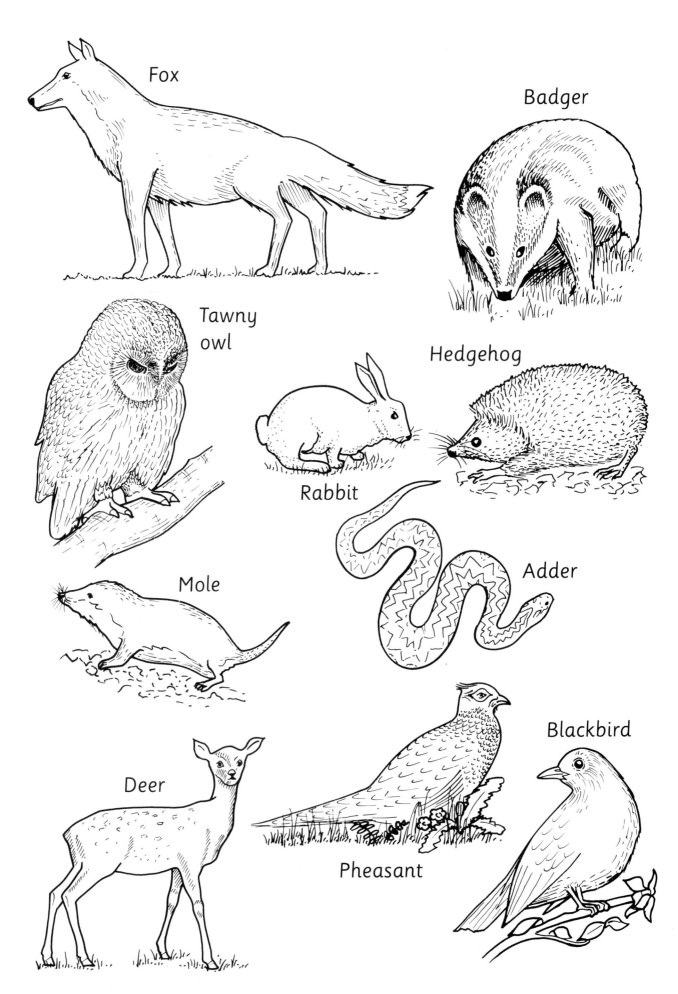

Fox

Badger

Tawny
owl

Hedgehog

Rabbit

Mole

Adder

Blackbird

Deer

Pheasant

Hut, Africa

Longhouse, Borneo

Lapp tents

Bamboo house, India

Mud houses, Turkey

Chalet, Switzerland

Farmhouse, Japan

Sheep farm, Australia

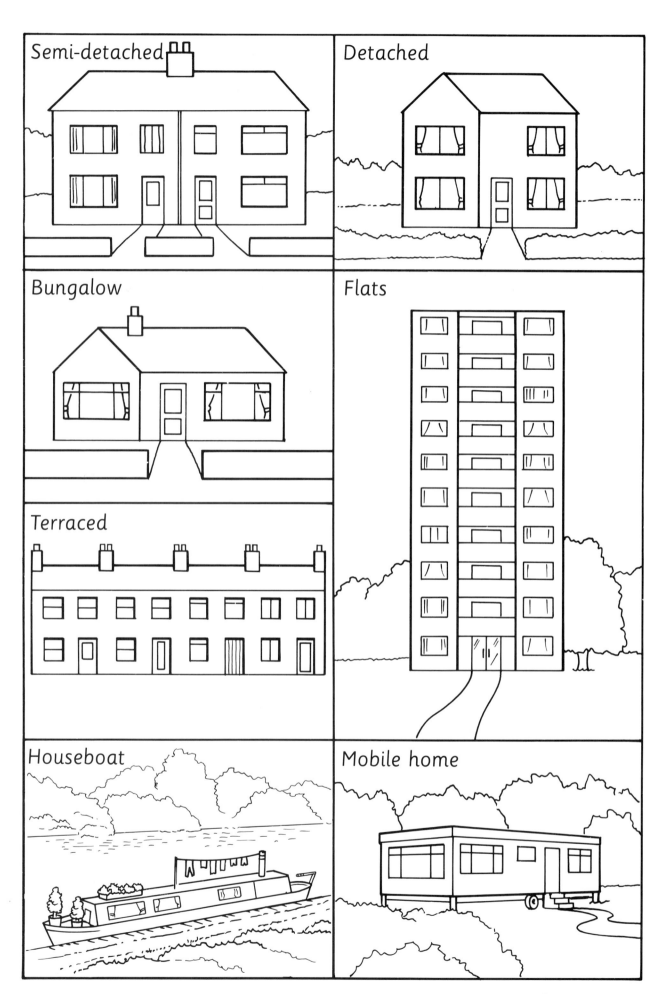

Semi-detached

Detached

Bungalow

Flats

Terraced

Houseboat

Mobile home

Minibeasts

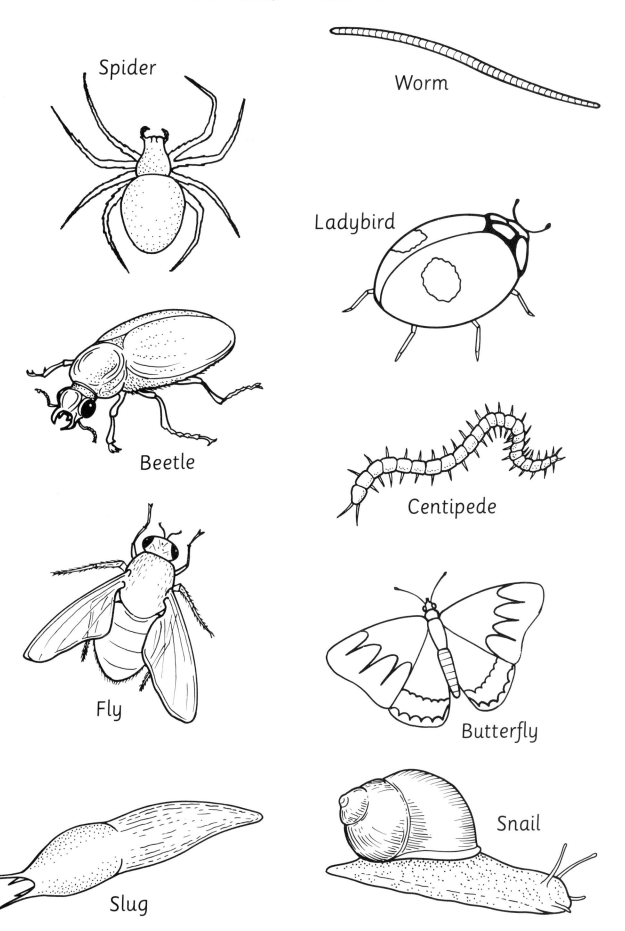

Spider

Worm

Ladybird

Beetle

Centipede

Fly

Butterfly

Slug

Snail

Dinosaurs

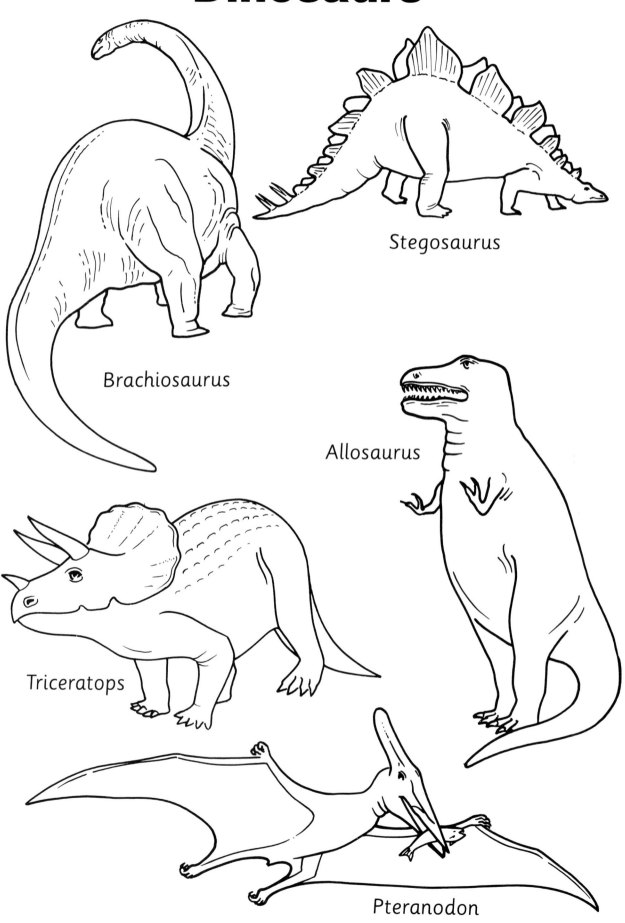

Stegosaurus

Brachiosaurus

Allosaurus

Triceratops

Pteranodon

Transport 1

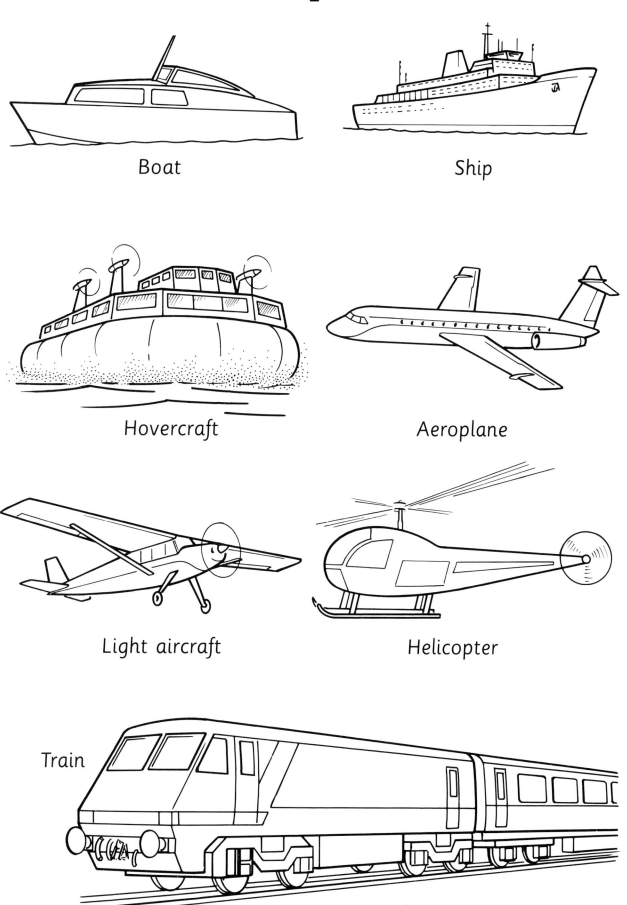

Boat

Ship

Hovercraft

Aeroplane

Light aircraft

Helicopter

Train

Transport 2

Bus

Coach

Van

Car

Motor bike

Bicycle

Lorry

Scientist

Milkman

Postperson

Fireman

Cook

Factory worker

Builder

Hairdresser

Teacher

Butcher

Doctor

Nurse

Ambulance
technician

Dustbin man

Dentist

Shop assistant

Policewoman

Compass points

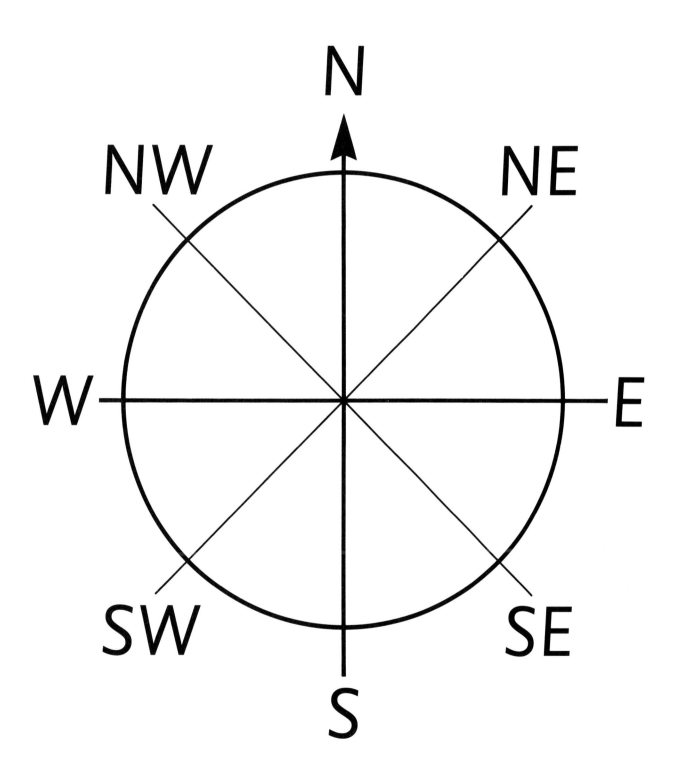

The British Isles

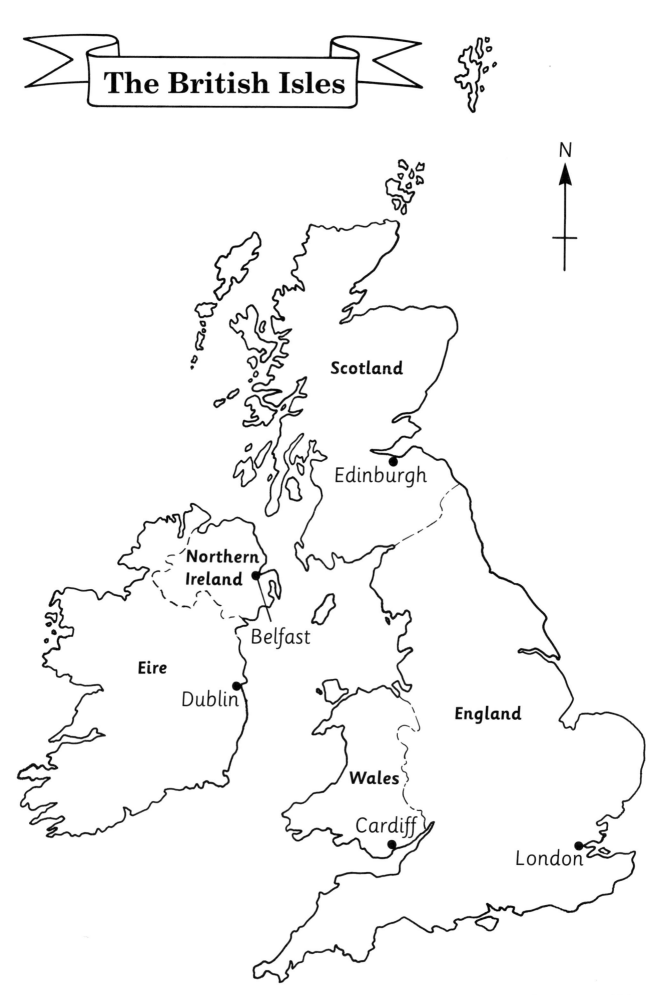

N

Scotland

Edinburgh

Northern
Ireland

Belfast

Eire

Dublin

England

Wales

Cardiff

London

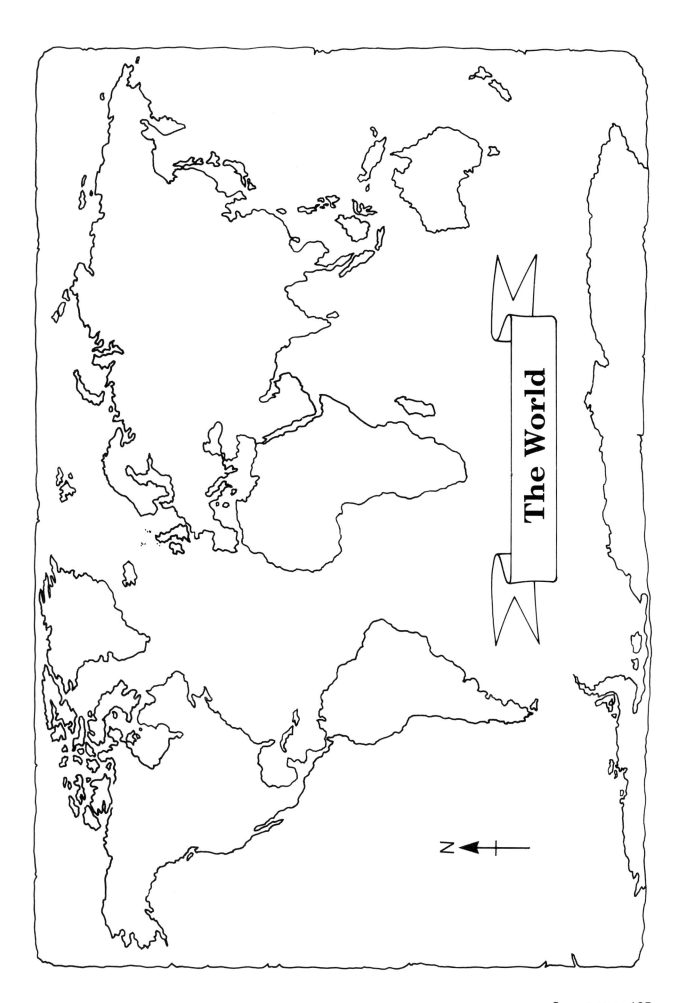

The World

N

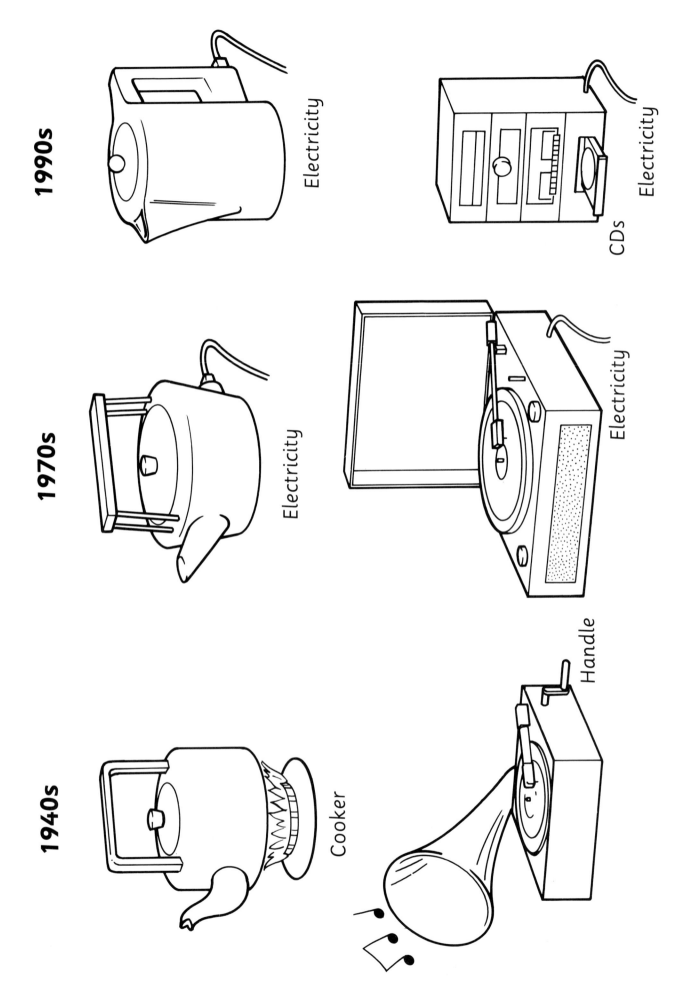

1990s

1970s

1940s

Electricity

Electricity

Electricity

Electricity

CDs

Cooker

Handle

1990s

Vauxhall Corsa

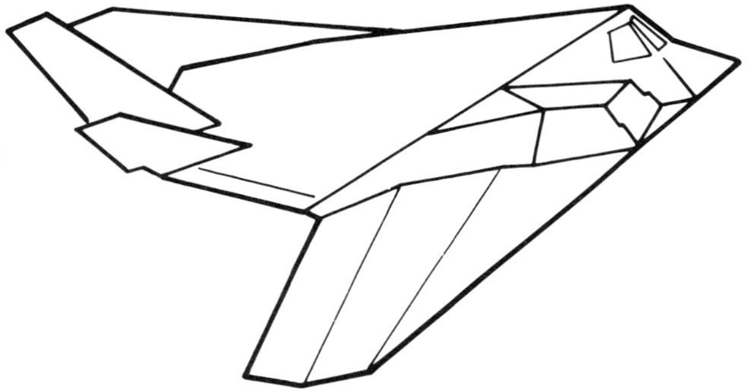

Stealth bomber

1970s

Mini

Boeing 747

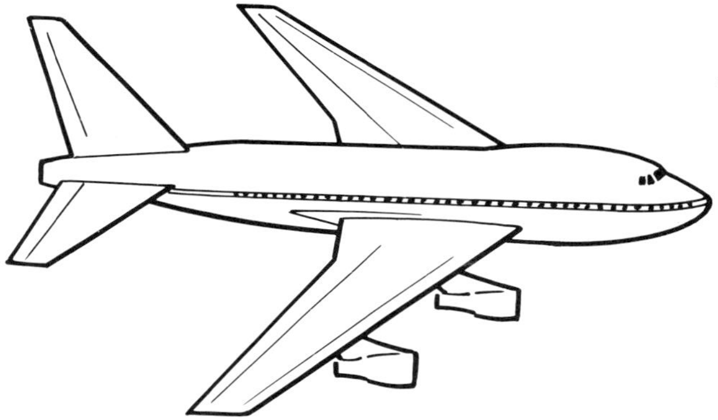

1940s

Austin 7

Spitfire

1990s

Designer detached house

New terraces

1970s

Flats

Semi-detached dormer bungalows

1940s

Prefabs

Bay window detached house

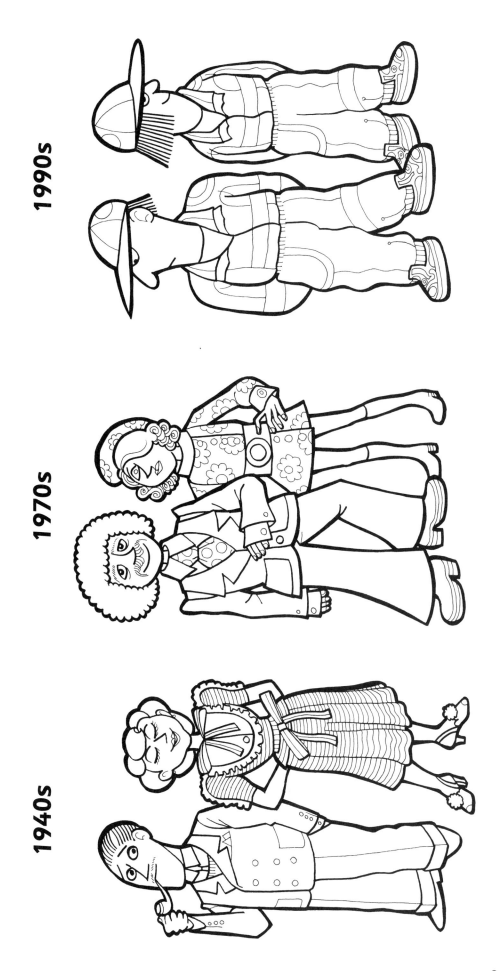

1990s

1970s

1940s

1940s

Tractor

Thresher

1970s

Tractor

Combine harvester

1990s

Tractor

Combine harvester

The Senses

 taste

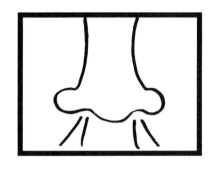 smell

 hearing

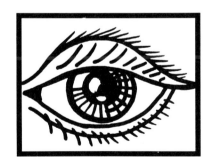 sight

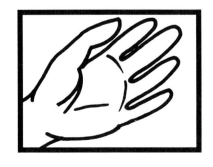 touch

Parts of a plant

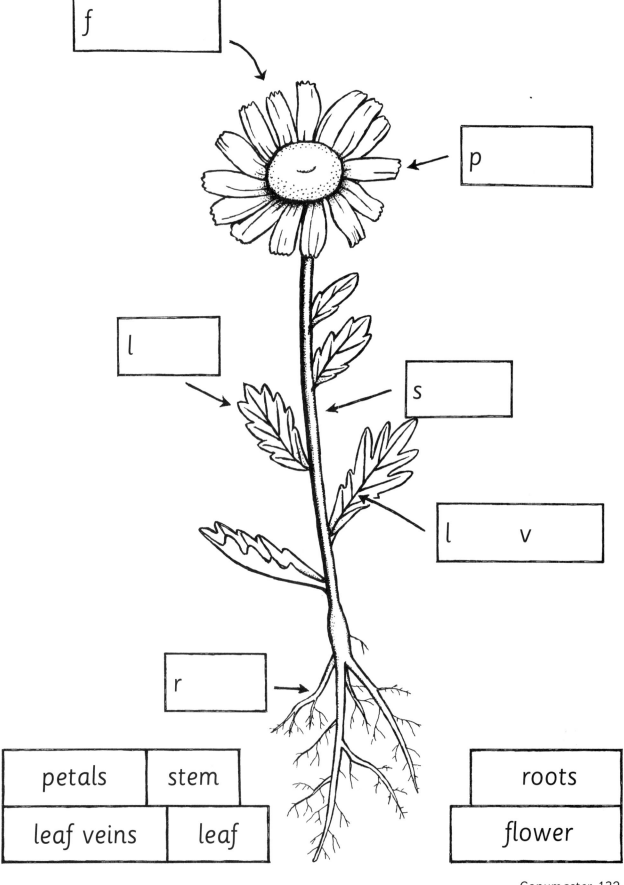

f

p

l

s

l   v

r

petals	stem
leaf veins	leaf

roots
flower

Animal homes

sett

warren

nest

holt

drey

den

fox

rabbit

otter

badger

blackbird

squirrel

Garden and wild flowers

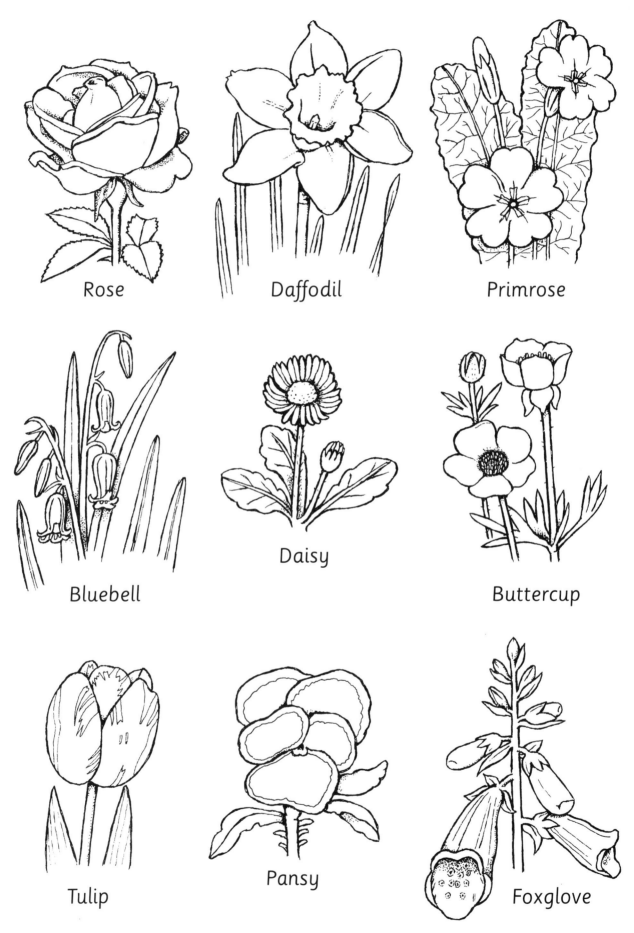

Rose

Daffodil

Primrose

Bluebell

Daisy

Buttercup

Tulip

Pansy

Foxglove

Common trees and their leaves

Oak

Beech

Lime

Sycamore

Ash

Holly

Farm animals

cow

pig

chicken

duck

sheep

turkey

dog

cat

Power sources

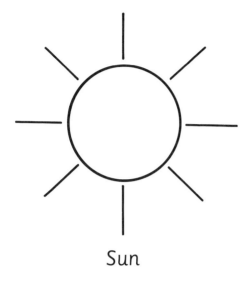

Sun

Gas

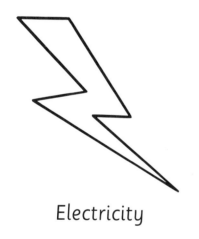

Electricity

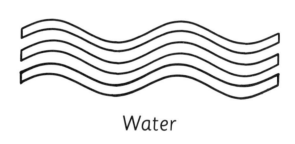

Water

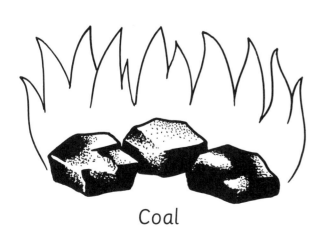

Coal

Nuclear

Earth in space

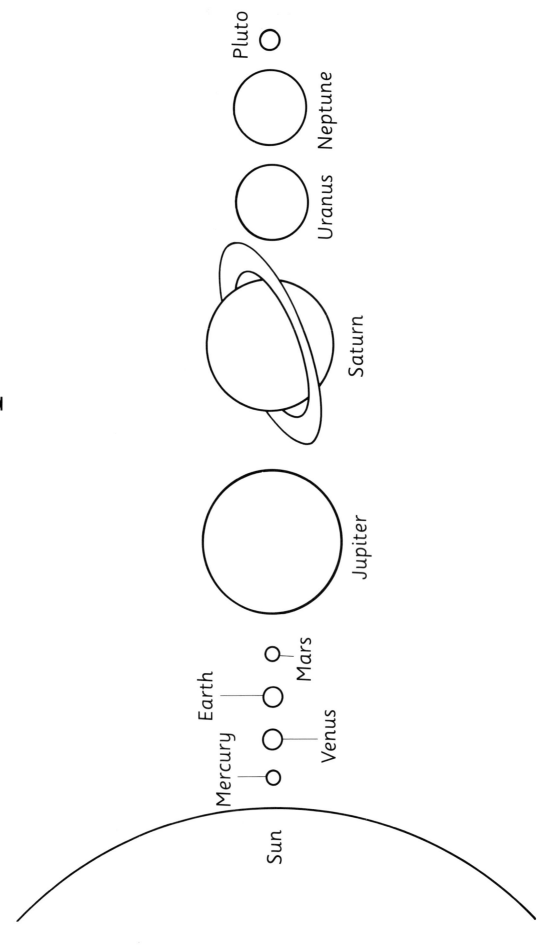

Sun

Mercury

Earth

Venus

Mars

Jupiter

Saturn

Uranus

Neptune

Pluto

Space

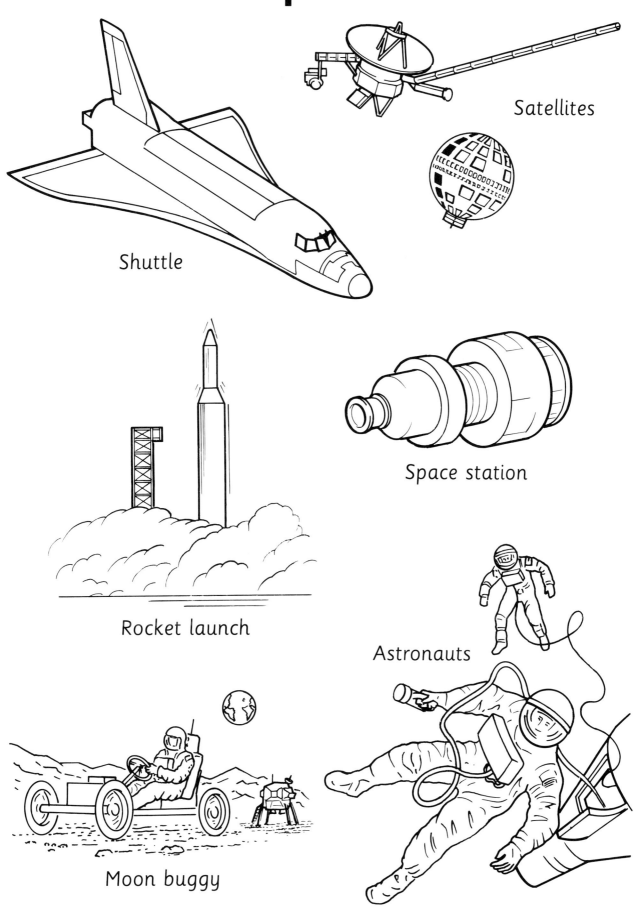

Shuttle

Satellites

Rocket launch

Space station

Astronauts

Moon buggy

Electrical items

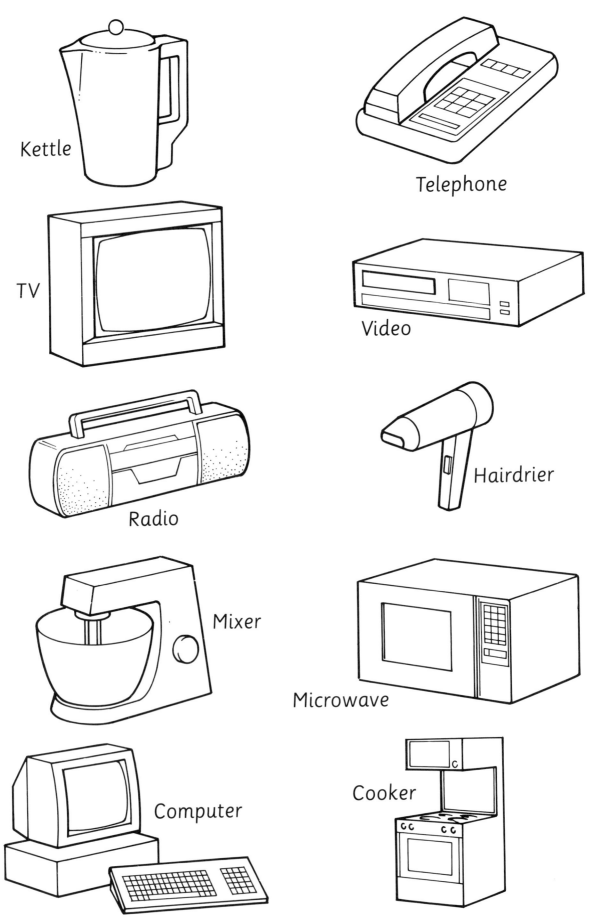

Kettle

Telephone

TV

Video

Radio

Hairdrier

Mixer

Microwave

Computer

Cooker

The open body

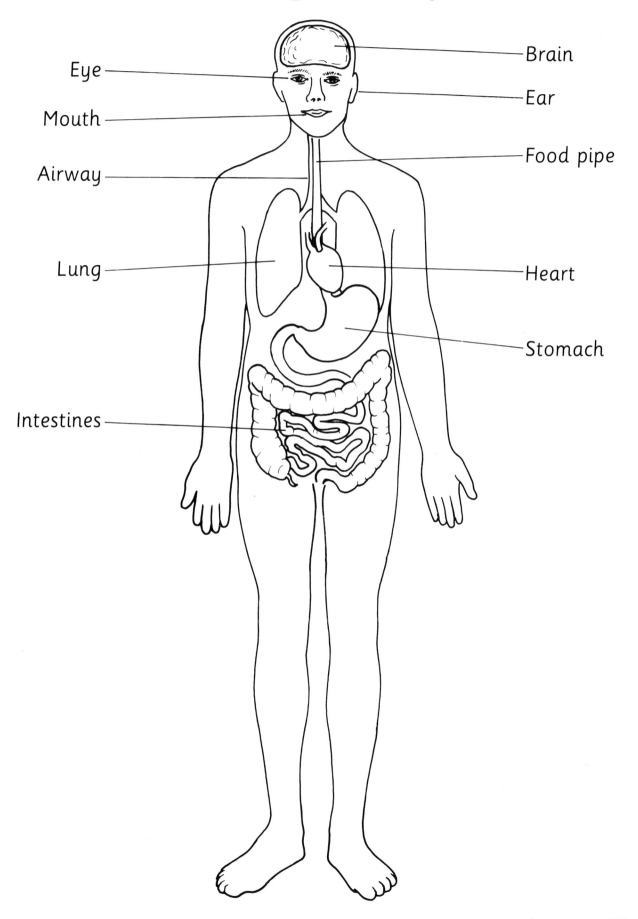

Eye

Mouth

Airway

Lung

Intestines

Brain

Ear

Food pipe

Heart

Stomach

The human skeleton

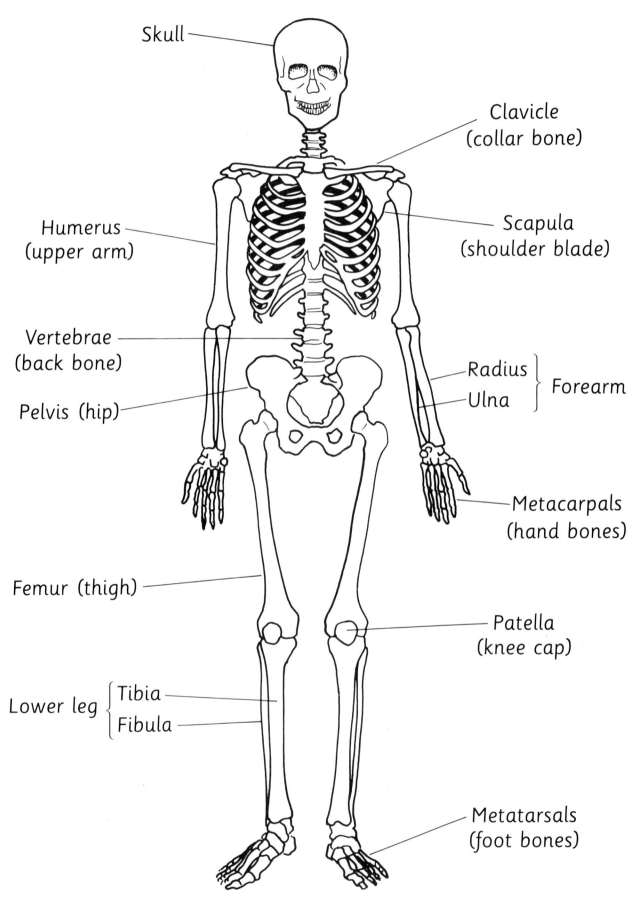

Skull

Clavicle
(collar bone)

Humerus
(upper arm)

Scapula
(shoulder blade)

Vertebrae
(back bone)

Radius

Forearm

Ulna

Pelvis (hip)

Metacarpals
(hand bones)

Femur (thigh)

Patella
(knee cap)

Lower leg { Tibia
Fibula

Metatarsals
(foot bones)

Musical instruments

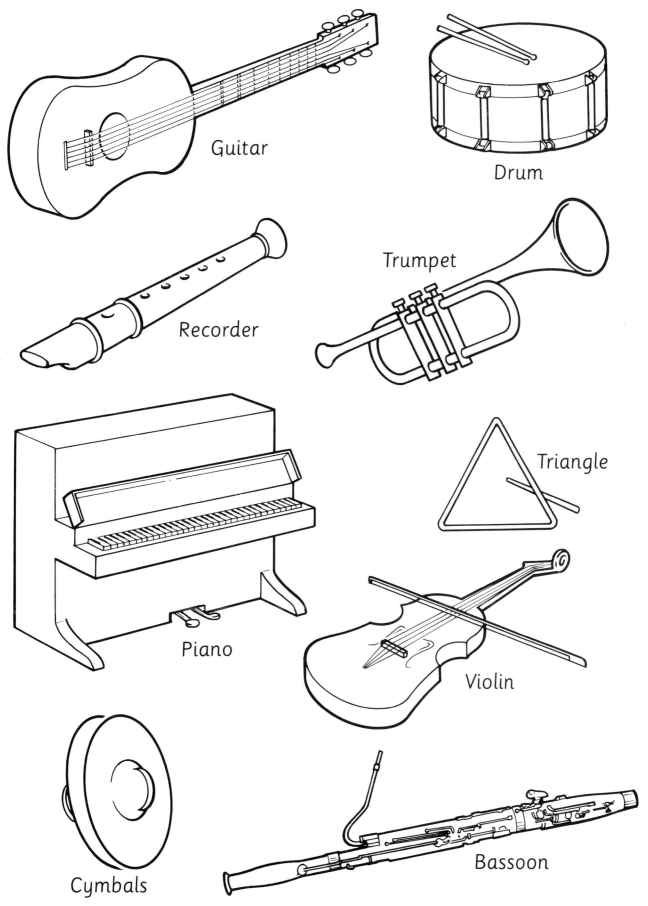

Guitar

Drum

Recorder

Trumpet

Piano

Triangle

Violin

Cymbals

Bassoon

Colours of the rainbow

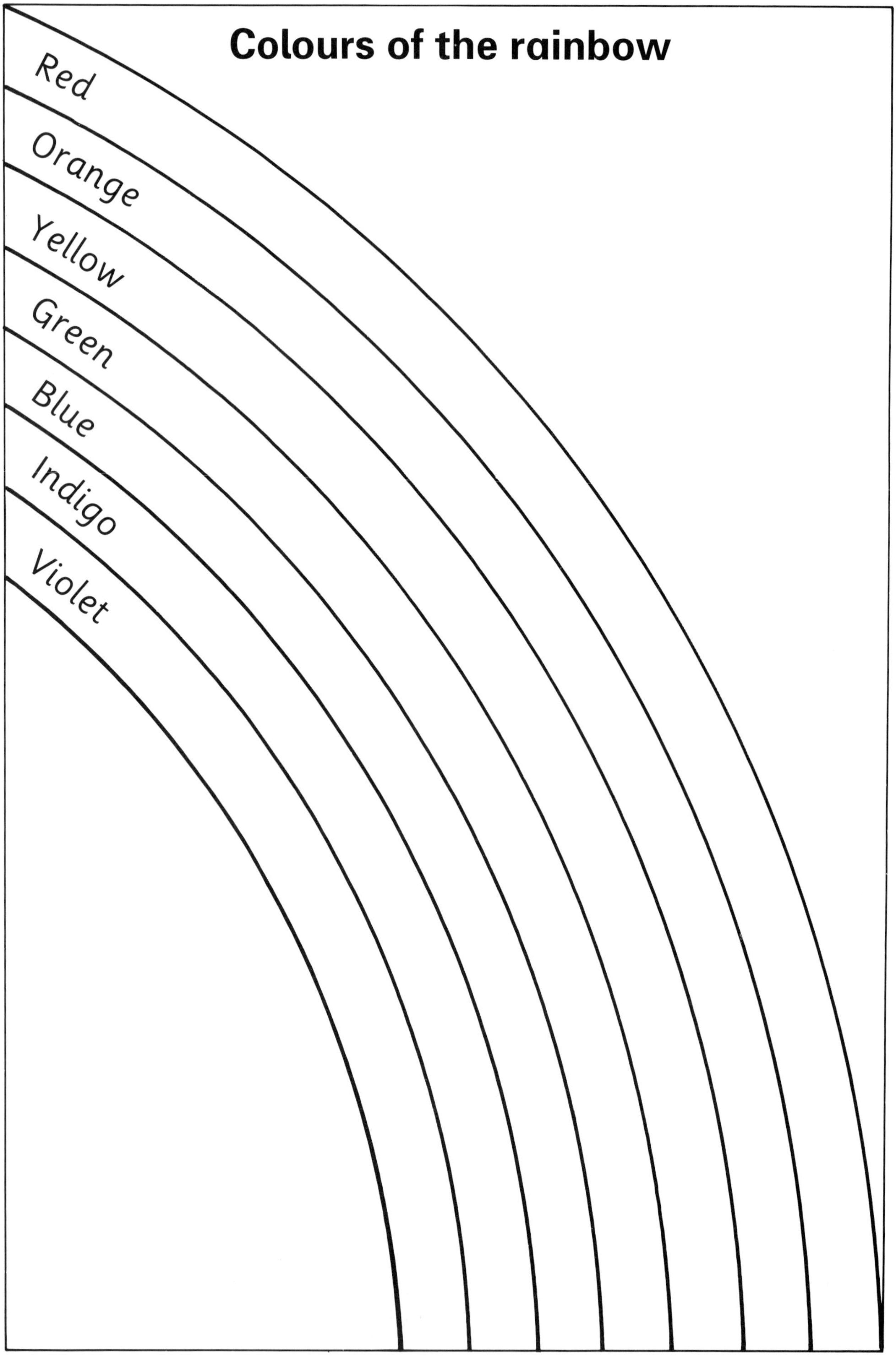

Red

Orange

Yellow

Green

Blue

Indigo

Violet

A special event in school

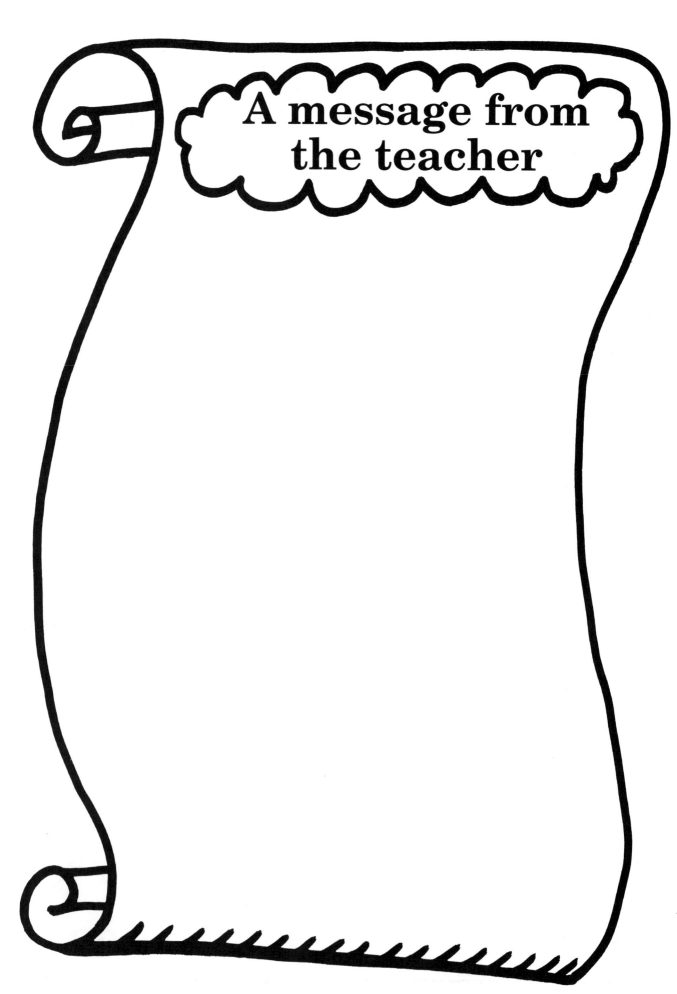

A message from the teacher

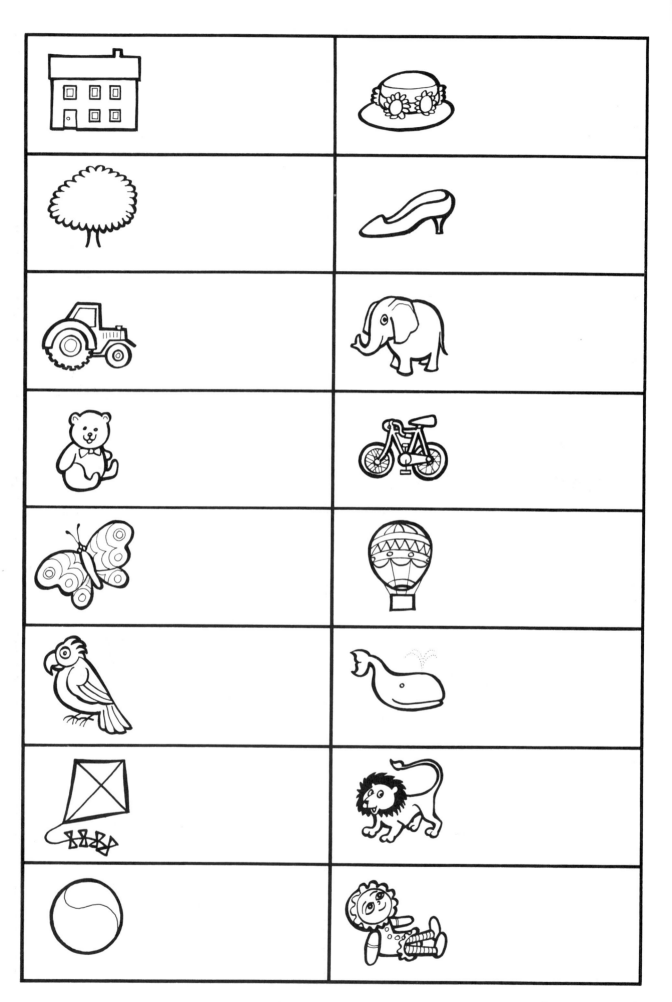

Good work

Super

WELL DONE

Excellent

Quiet worker

splendid

Good try **!**

very neat

This
certificate is
awarded for

_____

to _____

date _____ signed _____

Merit certificate

awarded to

_____

by _____

date _____